100

the Intimate Life

the Intimate Life

AWAKENING TO THE SPIRITUAL ESSENCE IN YOURSELF AND OTHERS

Judith Blackstone, PhD

SOUNDS TRUE
Boulder, Colorado

Sounds True
Boulder CO 80306

© 2011 Judith Blackstone

Sounds True is a trademark of Sounds True, Inc.

Published 2011

Cover and book design by Karen Polaski
Cover image © Erena.Wilson/Shutterstock

Printed in Canada

Library of Congress Cataloging-in-Publication Data
Blackstone, Judith, 1947–
  The intimate life : awakening to the spiritual essence in
yourself and others / Judith Blackstone.
  p. cm.
  ISBN 978-1-60407-562-5 (alk. paper)
  1. Spiritual life. 2. Love—Religious aspects. 3. Intimacy
(Psychology)—Religious aspects. I. Title.
  BL204'.4—DC22
  2011014095

eBook ISBN 978-1-60407-647-9

10 9 8 7 6 5 4 3 2 1

For Zoran,
with love for your pilgrim soul

Contents

INTRODUCTION
The Essential Unity
of Self and Other

TO LOVE LIFE, and in particular, to love other human beings, is one of the central ideals of every spiritual tradition. It is also one of life's greatest challenges. It requires the ability for true contact. And contact requires us to be authentic and deeply in touch with ourselves.

Every aspect of ourselves is capable of contact. We can contact another human being with our touch, gaze, and voice—and even with the subtle vibrations of our emotions, physical sensations, and awareness. We all crave this contact instinctively, for everything that it reaches becomes awake, alive.

The question addressed in this book is how we can deepen this capacity for contact, how we can become more adept at love. By love, I do not just mean love between intimate partners, but the warm, dynamic response of our heart to the world around us. The spiritual traditions teach that love is a basic component of the spiritual dimension. In the dualistic religions of the West, God is love. In the nondual traditions of the East, love is inherent in the spiritual essence that we can realize as our own being. Love is part of our own essential nature, somehow hidden or enfolded within us. Our desire and our efforts to love uncover our mysterious wound of separation from this authentic core of life. For this reason, our relationships can become spiritual pathways; they can help us realize the spiritual essence of ourselves.

For many people, the word "spiritual" suggests an intangible, inaccessible, and perhaps improbable realm of existence. As spirituality is understood in this book, however, the spiritual refers to our true and basic nature, beneath the fantasies, artifices, and constraints that distort our usual experience. It is our most subtle and most clear attunement to ourselves and the world around us. When we enter the spiritual path, we are becoming real.

Although it cannot be detected by the ordinary range of our senses, the subtle essence of our being does become tangible as we attune to it. It becomes an actual experience, a quality of being that is felt in our whole body and that can then be discerned in all of life. As we realize this essence of ourselves, our senses themselves become more subtle and begin to reveal the radiance, fluidity, and a spacious stillness that suffuses the material world. The most radical transformation that occurs with this subtle attunement is that instead of experiencing ourselves as separate from our environment, we find that our own being is continuous with everything around us. This book describes how the realization of this unified, spiritual dimension of life transforms all of our relationships.

The understanding that I present in this book is most closely aligned with the Hindu system of Advaita (nondual) Vedanta and the Tibetan Buddhist schools of Mahamudra and Dzog-chen. These Asian traditions have in common the recognition of a fundamental dimension of consciousness that encompasses and pervades all of our experience. Some of these traditions consider this dimension to be the nature of the mind, and some the nature of the universe. Some consider it to be the foundation of our individual minds, and others regard it as a unified dimension, as one mind at the root of all life. But they all agree that this dimension of pure consciousness is "uncreated." It spontaneously appears. It reveals itself to us as a transparency of our own being and everything around us.

My views are also informed by the accumulated knowledge of Western psychology and by old and new methods of body/mind healing. But the primary sources of the ideas and practices offered here are my own experience of spiritual practice, the necessities of my own healing, the challenges and gifts of my relationships, and the spontaneous emergence of guidance in response to the needs of my students and clients in my practice as a psychotherapist and spiritual teacher over the past three decades. I am not concerned with arguing for a particular philosophy, for I do not believe we can know for certain which explanation of ultimate reality is true. I do know that the experience of spiritual oneness is the innate potential of our human organism, and that it involves a transformation of every aspect of ourselves, including our physical body and our psychological maturity.

Spiritual realization is not a matter of constructing something new; it is always a clearing away, a letting go of the holding patterns and beliefs that obscure our true nature. If oneness is our true nature, it is also the natural potential, the underlying reality, of our relationships with other people. This book looks at how relationships can help both partners in a relationship release their barriers to spiritual oneness. This is presented as a dual process of resolving our resistances to contact with our partner and attuning directly to the subtle dimension of spiritual unity.

The spiritual essence of life is our most subtle, fundamental dimension of consciousness. The Asian literature describes fundamental consciousness as all-pervasive. It is experienced (or experiences itself) as vast space, pervading our own form and everything else that we experience, even physical space itself. It is therefore the basis of unity within our own being, our internal wholeness. And it is the basis of the unity of our own being with everything around us. It is an unbroken dimension, a dimension of wholeness and stillness that, when we attune to it, is coexistent with the movement of life. Spiritual realization is not just a matter of uplifting our mood or changing our behaviors and beliefs. It means that we enter into and experience ourselves as the spiritual foundation of existence.

Although the traditional teachings do not speak of it in this way, fundamental consciousness is the basis of contact: our deepest contact with ourselves, with other people, and with all of nature. It touches and knows everything that it pervades. Although our fundamental dimension of consciousness is referred to in spiritual teachings, it is just beginning to gain recognition in the psychological field. Up until recently, it was thought, in the more adventurous schools of psychology, physics, and medicine, that energy was the basic stratum of life. Energy, which is movement, such as flow, pulsation, or vibration, is easier to perceive and to feel than consciousness. The energy dimension is a spectrum in itself, from denser to subtler vibrations. When we realize ourselves as fundamental consciousness, we also reach the most subtle aspect of the energy spectrum. But we can experience the movement of energy without accessing the pervasive stillness of fundamental consciousness. Therefore, the application of fundamental consciousness to psychological and physical healing represents the cutting edge of the human growth movement.

There is also a growing recognition in contemporary psychology of the mutuality, or interconnectedness, of existence. The psychoanalytic theorist Robert D. Stolorow describes human interaction as an "intersubjective field" of mutual influence. Interestingly, in his book *Nonduality,* the Buddhist philosopher David Loy refers to the unified, spiritual dimension as a "pre-subjective ground," because it exists beyond, or deeper than, our subjective distortion of reality. In this book, I describe how the intersubjective field can gradually transform into the "pre-subjective" field of spiritual oneness. I also show how this shift brings compassion and insight to relationships, and helps both partners disentangle themselves from the defenses and projections that obstruct the flow of exchange between them.

Human development can be seen as a gradual realization of the oneness of self and other. As we evolve in this way, we develop inward contact and the capacity for contact with other people at the same time. It begins in infancy, as the rudimentary distinction between self-awareness and awareness of our mother (or primary caretaker), and culminates in the simultaneous self-knowledge and oneness with others that defines spiritual maturity. This book looks at the difficulties that thwart this developmental process and how they can lead to the boundary problems of merging (loss of self-contact) and distancing from others. It also shows how the realization of fundamental consciousness resolves these difficulties, so that our development toward spiritual oneness can proceed.

One of the main barriers to contact in intimate relationships is the fear that we will become submerged in another person. Attunement to fundamental consciousness can alleviate this fear because it pervades both our internal being and our environment as a unified whole. When we live in this dimension, we have a felt sense of both our internal experience and our oneness with the life around us. We can therefore experience oneness with another person while remaining attuned to our own internal being. Spiritual oneness is not a loss of self in the other, not the merging of identities that is so often a problem for people in relationships. It is the unity and continuity of two individual people. In the dimension of our spiritual essence, we grow simultaneously toward wholeness within our own body and oneness with other people.

In this book, I present several ways that couples can enter into the oneness of fundamental consciousness together. One of the ways is through a subtle channel that runs through the vertical core of the body. This channel is the center of the chakra system in Hindu Yoga and is called *sushumna*. In Buddhism, it is called "the central channel."

To find this subtle core of the body, you can focus inward toward your spine from the front of your body, as deeply as you can without strain. Finding the subtle core of the body requires not just depth of focus, but also subtlety. It is a subtle inward attunement to ourselves. The sushumna forms a straight line from the top of your head to the center of the bottom of your torso. It cannot be neatly equated with any part of our physical anatomy, such as the spine, for a normal spine is not a straight line. Instead, it needs to be located through the "feel" of it. It has an electrical quality, a subtle vibratory "buzz." The subtle core of our body is both our deepest connection with ourselves and the basis of our oneness with other people. In the dimension of spiritual oneness, partners can relate with each other "core-to-core." This releases a flow of subtle energies between them, which provides a nonverbal foundation for communication.

Another way that couples can enter into fundamental consciousness together is by attuning to the essential qualities of this dimension. Fundamental consciousness can be experienced as emptiness, as the clear-through transparency of our own body and of everything that we experience in our environment. When two people attune to this pervasive emptiness together, they experience a mutual transparency of themselves and each other.

But fundamental consciousness can also be attuned to as presence. This presence aspect of fundamental consciousness is not simply empty; it is rich with the essential qualities of being. In this book,

I divide the presence aspect of fundamental consciousness into three qualities: awareness, emotion, and physical sensation. These are ongoing, unchanging qualities; they make up the unchanging stillness of our spiritual dimension. Specific and constantly changing awarenesses, emotions, and physical sensations arise and end within this unchanging ground of our being.

Awareness, emotion, and physical sensation are also the three major pathways of our contact with other people. As we realize the spiritual foundation of life, we experience contact with other people as a continuity of these three essential qualities. Most people have more access to some of these qualities than others. For example, they may be able to experience emotional contact with another human being, but physical sensation is more difficult. When two people feel out of contact with each other, or when they reach an impasse in their communication, it is often because they are each open to different aspects of contact. But fundamental consciousness is a dimension of wholeness. When we realize this subtle ground, we can connect with other people through all three pathways at once. Also, the process of two people opening to each other in the realms of sensation, emotion, and awareness can facilitate the realization of spiritual oneness for both of them.

The realization of fundamental consciousness gradually transforms the functioning of our senses. It is as if our senses are washed clean of our habitual ways of focusing on the world, and stripped of the mental elaborations that usually accompany our perceptions. If we look at a flower, for example, we do not get caught up in naming the kind of flower it is, or in our particular preference for this kind or another, but rather we experience fully this particular flower in this particular moment: its texture, its color and shape, its fragrance, its "flowerness." The traditional spiritual literature of the East calls this "direct" or "bare" perception. We feel that, for the first time, we are perceiving the world as it really is. Our senses also become more refined, and, as I have said, they reveal a more subtle world. Everything that we perceive appears to be made of energy and consciousness.

The experience of bare perception is part of our oneness with other people. Usually, we see and touch only from the surface of ourselves to the surface of other people. But in fundamental consciousness, we are able to see, hear, and touch beneath the surface to the feelings and qualities within. We are able to hear the qualities of a person's whole being in the sound of their voice and to feel these qualities in the sensation of their touch. Bare perception can provide the basis of deep understanding and attunement.

Spiritual oneness also brings a deepened perspective and compassion to one of the main challenges of intimacy—coping with childhood wounds and defenses, our own and those of our partner, that become activated by intimate relationships. In the clear, pervasive space of fundamental consciousness, it becomes easier to recognize and release the defenses, beliefs, and behaviors that prevent us from experiencing contact with another person.

Our psychological defenses are not just mental; they are ways that we constricted our bodies when we were children in order to lessen the impact of painful experience. They are ways that we shaped ourselves—body, heart, and mind—in order to be loved and to feel safe within our childhood families. The defensive constrictions in our body prevent us from fully embodying ourselves, from fully contacting the internal space of our bodies. Wherever we cannot contact our own internal being, we are not available for contact with other people. As we become more in contact with ourselves and others, we also become more open to the spiritual dimension of life.

Attunement to fundamental consciousness also helps release the psychological constrictions that diminish sexual pleasure. Physical sensation is an inseparable part of the essence of our being and of our spiritual oneness with other life. The limitation that many people experience in their capacity for sexual pleasure is also a barrier to the realization of spiritual oneness.

In some Tantric traditions, partners use the energy of sexual release to "fuel" the rise of energy through their bodies. These exercises usually involve ways that partners can circulate their breath and energy systems. In chapter 7, this book describes how partners can include fundamental consciousness in their sexual practice to reach an even deeper level of contact with each other and to facilitate the most profound level of spiritual realization.

There are exercises at the end of each chapter that will help you practice relating with other people in the dimension of spiritual oneness. They include ways for partners to directly experience the clear, unified space of fundamental consciousness, to contact each other from the core of their bodies, to experience the continuity of love, awareness, and physical sensation, and to refine their senses so that they can see, hear, and touch each other on a more subtle level. There are also exercises that combine traditional Tantric energy exercises with attunement to fundamental consciousness during sexual union.

These exercises are from the Realization Process, a method that I have developed over the past thirty years. Unlike most traditional spiritual techniques, the Realization Process focuses directly both on awakening spiritual essence in our whole body and on relating with other people while remaining in this essence.

Traditionally, spiritual transformation has been taught as a solitary practice, even requiring the avoidance of social attachments and commitments. This book views the true meaning of spiritual detachment as the ability to allow life to flow without manipulation or defense. This means that we need to be fully open and available in our reception and response to life. Since our defensive strategies and rigidities were formed in relationship to other people, relationships are the ideal context for releasing those defenses.

If we do not include relationships in our spiritual practice, we often lose our realization as soon as we encounter another human being. But if we have practiced relating with other people in fundamental consciousness, we can maintain our spiritual realization in our daily lives, so that it is not a temporary peak experience, but a lasting transformation of consciousness.

Fundamental consciousness is a relational field, a unity of self and other. When we attempt to shut out either our environment or our internal life, we fragment our own consciousness, and this conceals our essence. Spiritual oneness is the absolute balance of inward and outward contact. It is the deepest contact we can have with our own self and with everyone and everything that we encounter. It means that we are able to see through the surface of people and things to their essence. When we touch a plant or an animal or another human being, we can feel the streaming of the life force and the responsiveness of the subtle intelligence and love within them. We can experience that our own essence of sensation, love, and awareness resonates with the same essential qualities of everything around us.

In the dimension of fundamental consciousness, intimate partners begin to know each other, to experience each other, through the whole internal depth of their being. This is immensely satisfying, because it is the goal of our driving hunger for contact with other life. This contact—the ability to feel genuine love for another person, to experience the mental excitement of two minds meeting and the pleasure of unguarded physical sensation—is among the greatest rewards of spiritual awakening.

I

the RELATIONAL FIELD
Attuning to Unified Consciousness

*It is one and the same Self that shines as one's
own self as well as the selves of others.*

VIJNANABHAIRAVA

THE ONENESS of the spiritual dimension is the underlying reality of all relationships. It can be described as a relational field, a fundamental continuity of self and other. In the spaciousness and stillness of our spiritual essence, we are truly in contact, truly intimate, with ourselves and with all of life.

The idea that people are interconnected in a relational field is in agreement with the contemporary view of the world as an open "system" in which all parts influence the others. In the field of psychology, the theory of "intersubjectivity" describes relationships as interactions of differently organized subjective worlds.[1] The relational field described in this book, however, is more subtle than the field of interacting subjectivities. It is experienced as a fundamental, unified dimension of consciousness.

The spiritual essence of life is beyond our rigid subjective modification of experience. To the extent that we are either consciously or unconsciously manipulating ourselves and our relationship with the world, we do not experience our fundamental oneness with other people. As we let go of rigid or fixed organizations of the way we experience ourselves and others, we uncover a dimension of unity between ourselves and other life. Spiritual maturity can be seen as the realization of the fundamental unity of the relational field.

The various schools of Asian spiritual philosophy have different ways of describing ultimate reality, or fundamental consciousness, but they point to the same experience of unity. For example, Sankara, the revered teacher of Hindu nondualism, writes, "I fill all things, inside and out, like space. Changeless and the same in all, I am pure, unattached, stainless, and immutable."[2]

A Buddhist text from the Dzog-chen tradition says, "Within naturally occurring timeless awareness, a single basic space, all things are present in such a way that they are in essence nondual."[3]

Spiritual realization is a process of laying bare this underlying reality. It is a process of dissolving the subjective limitations and distortions of our essential being.

However, the Asian spiritual traditions also teach that the complete realization of fundamental consciousness is extremely rare. In fact, it may be that no one is completely realized, that the nature of embodied existence is always, to some extent, limited and subjective. But it is also clear, from observing the progression of spiritual realization, that we mature in the direction of ultimate reality.

Although absolute oneness appears to be virtually unattainable in its entirety, it is not hypothetical. It is a dimension of ourselves that is unmistakable once we attune to it. It is an experiential and observable reality. It is a dimension of consciousness that transcends—that releases the constraints of—our own subjectivity.

This is not a negation of our humanness. The experience of existing as a human being, of being alive to ourselves and the world around us, of responding to life with insight, emotion, and sensation, increases as we release our subjective organization. As we realize this undistorted, unified consciousness, we have a sense of becoming real and of experiencing life as it really is. When two people are both attuned to this dimension, they have a sense of being in genuine contact with each other.

The image of a relational field also represents the spatial nature of fundamental consciousness. This dimension of life is experienced as vast, empty space pervading everything, even physical space itself. When we attune to it, we feel that we are made of empty space. And we feel continuous with the empty space that everything else is made of. This is an actual change in the texture of our experience. Instead of feeling solid and separate, we feel permeable, and everything around us also appears to be permeable, transparent.

People often ask me what sort of experience this is. Is attunement to fundamental consciousness a sensation, a feeling, an awareness? Fundamental consciousness is the essence of our whole being, and it is known through our whole being. It is an integration—the integrative ground—of awareness, sensation, and emotion. Fundamental consciousness is said to be "self-reflecting" because it awakens to itself. It knows itself. This type of knowing is unlike any other. It is not an experience "of" something in the same way that we have an experience of a blue sky, or of a feeling of sadness, or of a sensation of heat. Fundamental consciousness is the knower itself, not an object of the knower. To experience fundamental consciousness means that the knower begins to know itself.

When two people are together attuned to the relational field, they feel continuous with each other as the empty space of fundamental consciousness. They experience that they are living in an unbounded field of unified presence.

Consciousness and Flow

Although the spiritual dimension of life is experienced as motion-less space, all of the content of experience is movement. Feelings move, thoughts move, our physiological systems all move, even circumstances move. We experience the stillness of fundamental consciousness and the dynamic flow of life at the same time. The more we attune to and become the stillness, the more the movement of life occurs without obstruction, without resistance or distortion. The content of experience is inseparable from the stillness of fundamental consciousness, in the same way that waves are inseparable from the ocean. Everything that we experience in the spiritual dimension appears to be made of the same subtle consciousness that experiences it.

Zen Buddhism describes the unobstructed movement of life as "leaving no trace." It passes through the stillness of our consciousness without our grasping or manipulating it and without disturbing or altering the stillness in any way. For example, if we feel sad, and we do not interfere with this feeling at all, it will register vividly in our consciousness and then dissipate. But if we try not to feel sad, we will have to clamp down on the spontaneous movement of experience by constricting our body and energy system, and this will actually maintain the experience of sadness within our organism. If we continue to prevent this emotion from moving, the holding pattern will become a chronic rigidity in our being. It will become an ongoing limitation in our ability to feel emotion. Any rigidity in our own being is also a barrier between ourselves and other people. The bound sadness will also color our experience, so that life always seems a little sad. For this reason, spiritual realization requires that we accept and experience life just as it is, in each moment.

To the extent that two people are both attuned to the still-ness of fundamental consciousness, the exchange between them moves with fluidity and spontaneity. In this clear, unified space, it becomes easier to recognize and dissolve the residual barriers of numbness, of bound fear, sadness, confusion, and anger that separate us from other people and impede this flow. When the flow of exchange between partners gets "stuck," we become aware of a locus for healing to take place that will help both people open to their spiritual essence.

The unity of self and other is our true nature. Once we have reached this dimension of ourselves, we experience unity even with people who have not realized fundamental consciousness. We experience that our own essence is continuous with theirs—that the spaciousness that pervades our own being also pervades them. Many people fear that they will be lonely if they attune more subtly to life than other people do. But this subtle attunement gives us a felt sense of kinship and connection with all other life.

The Body of Clear Space

We cannot truly understand human development—or the dimension of spiritual oneness—unless we understand how the body is involved in the process of spiritual realization. The body can be experienced as physical matter, as energy, or as consciousness. Our most subtle and clear experience of the body is that it is made of consciousness. This is the integration of body and mind. It means that we have inward contact with the whole internal space of our body. Although the total unity of body and mind is considered a very advanced and rare attainment,[4] we progress toward this integration as we realize fundamental consciousness.

Our experience of spiritual oneness is obstructed by static areas in our body and energy system. These are literally places within our organism where we are holding still against the flow of experience. Some of these patterns are chronic, or in other words, the tissues of the body have rigidified in the shape of the holding pattern. For example, if a child cringes every time she hears the angry voices of her parents, this unconscious, repeated reaction of her body may become a static contraction in her muscles and fascia. Other patterns are evoked by specific circumstances that remind us of painful events in our past. A child may, for example, cringe in response to her parents yelling, but this reaction does not happen often enough to become an ongoing contraction in her body. Instead, the cringe will be temporary but it may become a well-traveled groove that her body follows whenever she hears angry voices, or some similar threat, throughout the rest of her life. These holding patterns, especially those that are ongoing, impede and distort our contact with ourselves and with other people. They diminish our awareness, emotion, and sensation.

As I will explain more fully in the next chapter, spiritual realization is not just a return to the pre-defended state of infancy. But we do need to let go of our holding patterns in order for the process of human development to continue toward spiritual maturity. When we live in the dimension of fundamental consciousness, we are able to experience these held areas in our body as tensions within the fluidity of our experience or as densities within the clear space of our consciousness. Some people describe seeing them as patches of darkness within the luminosity of the spiritual dimension.

As we become one with the relational field of fundamental consciousness, the physical body becomes less rigid, less held in position. We have a sense of inhabiting the internal space of our body, of reclaiming the space that we had constricted in our defensive organizations. And we gain depth, range, and authenticity in our contact with the world around us.

Our somatic holding patterns are connected with static beliefs and repetitive behaviors. This can be illustrated by a woman named Sara, who came to work with me because she seemed unable to maintain an intimate relationship. She was extremely lonely, and, now in her late forties, she had begun to despair that she would ever find love. She told me that men always ended relationships with her just when she was beginning to feel really involved with them. When we met, Sara had just started going out with someone new, and she was afraid that the same pattern would repeat again.

When Sara described her isolation to me, I was surprised. She seemed to me a very warm, lively, and trusting woman. As she sat across from me, I could feel the movement of love in the space between us. But each time she mentioned one of the men she had known, the same shift occurred in her. I sensed a hardening deep inside her chest, and I could see the constriction in her eyes and brow. There was also a subtle upward displacement of her energy, so that her forehead became the dominant location of her presence, conveying a sense of superiority and judgment. This holding pattern stopped the flow of love in our relational field, just as it had in her relationships with men.

Sara herself was unaware of the shift that had taken place in her. So she was always confused and surprised when men responded to it with their own defenses and, finally, by leaving her. But when I pointed it out to her, she could feel it in her body, and she recognized it as a familiar movement.

In the Realization Process, there are specific methods for releasing these holding patterns. Since they are unconscious, the first step is to become conscious of them. The next step is to experience the purpose of the holding pattern, to feel what it is protecting against or what it is holding back, such as tears or anger. This allows us to become aligned with the volitional intention of the movement, so that it is not something that is happening to us, but we recognize that we ourselves are moving toward this protective stance. This is not necessarily a postural change. It can take place within the internal space of the body, like Sara's hardening of her chest. Once the protective movement becomes conscious and intentional, we can practice allowing ourselves to move into the pattern and release it. Usually repeated practice is required in order for the pattern to release completely.

I asked Sara to shift into the contraction as she pictured one of the men from her past. When she did this, she recognized that she was trying not to love him. When she pictured the same man and allowed the contraction to release, she felt longing for him, then fear that he would reject her, and then grief that the relationship had ended.

As she allowed herself to feel this pain, she remembered that her father had suddenly become withdrawn from her when she was about five years old. He was often not home in the evenings, as he had been before, and when he was home, he seemed less affectionate toward her. Sara also remembered that her mother was very critical of her father at around this time. She could picture her mother scolding her father as if he were a child, while he withdrew into stony silence. In order to cope with the heartache of her father's withdrawal, she had shut down her own loving response toward him. At the same time, she had imitated her mother's critical attitude. This imitation of attitude, which psychologists call "introjection," is an unconscious mirroring of a parent's (or caretaker's) subjective organization. It is not just an imitation of behavior, but of the subjective organization of the whole organism.

I then asked Sara to imagine her father in front of her. Sara was able to observe that she automatically closed her heart as she pictured him. As she gradually released this holding pattern, she was able to feel her deep grief at the loss of his love. After this session, Sara practiced keeping her heart open in her relationship with the new man in her life. Although she still went into her familiar holding pattern at times, she could recognize the shift as it occurred and let go of it. She also understood that this holding pattern signaled that she was feeling vulnerable because she was feeling love.

The shifts in the organization of our body and energy system are usually so subtle that they go unnoticed. When therapists work with couples, it is important that they watch specifically for where the relational field is open or closed between the partners, and how this changes as they discuss their relationship. When a therapist works with an individual, these same shifts occur in the relational field between them, as the individual describes current difficulties and the important events of the past. This subtle "dance of veils" is the key to understanding the problematic areas of a person's life and helping them open to their spiritual essence.

The Authentic Self

We realize the dimension of spiritual oneness through subtle, inward attunement to our own body. It is a paradox of nature that the more inward contact we have with our own form, the more we experience oneness with other life. Wherever we inhabit our own body, we become permeable. We can experience the present moment occurring inside and outside of our body at the same time. This means that the transcendence (the openness) of our individual form and the inhabiting of our individual form occur at the same time. Our individual wholeness and our oneness with other life develop simultaneously, through the realization of fundamental consciousness.

As the barriers between ourselves and other people dissolve, we are able to feel more whole and intact within our own being. We experience an internal continuity of spiritual essence that seems to collect and "jell" within our body as our realization progresses. We can rest in our essence without having to support it in any way. We feel both intact within ourselves and entirely open, or transparent, entirely continuous with our environment. At this point, it requires no effort at all to live within our own body.

Spiritual realization is therefore synonymous with personal maturity. As we inhabit the internal space of our body, we awaken the inherent capacities of our being. For example, we develop our capacity for love, understanding, and physical pleasure, as well as the most subtle and accurate functioning of all our senses.

In Hindu nondual (Advaita) philosophy, fundamental consciousness is described as the one unified consciousness of the universe: a single self that is experienced as the primary self of all beings. This is similar to the Jewish mystical conception, which says that we are all sparks of a single flame. We are all embodiments of a single light, a single source of wisdom and love.

In Hindu philosophy, one of the names of fundamental consciousness is "Self." As I have said, this refers to the single self of all creation. But this term is not just a concept; it is also a qualitative description of our essence. We can enter the dimension of fundamental consciousness through attunement to the quality of self within the internal space of our body. Although it is difficult to describe this quality, I have found that when I ask people to attune to the quality of self, most people have no difficulty doing it.

You can test this out quickly yourself, if you wish, by taking a moment to feel that you inhabit the internal space of your arms. Now attune to the quality of your self inside your arms. Although this is not a quality that we usually notice, because it is the ground of life and not the content, it has always been there, as part of the feeling of being alive. Some people object to the word "self" in this context because it can easily be confused with the constructed self—the subjective organization of oneself—that conceals the reality of spiritual oneness. They suggest that I use the word "being." But interestingly, attunement to being does not bring us into as subtle a dimension of ourselves as attunement to self. Attuning to the quality of self evokes the spiritual dimension within the internal space of the body, and the dissolution of the barriers between internal and external experience. And attuning to the quality of self within just one part of the body—our arms, for example—brings us into the spiritual dimension within our entire body.

Attunement to the quality of self is an exercise or practice. The realization of our spiritual essence is a relaxed state; in fact, it is our most relaxed, natural state, not an action of any sort. But this exercise, and all of the exercises presented in this book, functions like a stretch for our consciousness, which eventually enables us to settle into this most subtle dimension of ourselves without any effort.

As I mentioned above, the quality of self is not the same as our many ideas about ourselves that make up what we might call our "false identity." Our false identity contains static images of ourselves—for example, an image of authority or an image of cheerfulness—that we have assumed to cope with the challenges of our particular life circumstances. They are part of our defensive holding pattern: subjective organizations that stop the flow of experience and obstruct our contact with our essence. Over time, these images harden within the tissues of the body, forming rigid personae that we can easily mistake for our true being. The false, rigid parts of ourselves can be difficult to recognize; they are often hard to give up because they are usually effective. Once other people are convinced by our persona, our interactions with them constantly reinforce our false-character structure. Then we feel locked into relationships that seem to require us to always be that cartoon of authority or that smiling happy face.

The authenticity of the self that occurs with spiritual realization is not just a shift in the way we experience ourselves. It can also be observed by other people as a transformation of the way we look and sound, even the quality of our touch. Although I have witnessed this transformation many times, it still seems to me as mysterious and amazing an aspect of nature as birth or death.

For example, a man named Leo has been coming to work with me for about five months. I do not know much about him. Although he is always warm and cordial, he does not talk about himself but likes to get right to the meditation exercises. He comes in, sits down and closes his eyes, and I lead him through the Realization Process. Then he opens his eyes and sometimes asks me a question about the work or reports on some new experience that he had that session. Then he gets up and leaves. Over the months I have watched him deepen, as if he were gradually materializing within his body. Then, two weeks ago, when he opened his eyes, there he was, looking out at me. It was an unmistakable shift, from the polite, veiled expression that he always wore to the unmasked, vital presence of a real person. I could see him, and though I still did not know many details about his life, I knew him.

Because our essence pervades our whole body, to become attuned to it means that we become alive throughout the whole internal depth of ourselves. In his novel *Fup,* Jim Dodge has a character say, "If you just stand still and *feel* for a moment you would know how everything yearns to be wild."[5] To live in the subtle, spiritual ground of ourselves is to arrive at our own wild existence.

We all have a natural ability to recognize authenticity. Just as we can tell balance from imbalance or harmony from dissonance, we are designed to detect the ring of truth. This capacity becomes increasingly acute as we realize fundamental consciousness. It is a navigational tool for guiding us toward the realization of our authentic, spiritual being. We also have a natural craving for authenticity. Although we may not know what we are missing, if we become too cut off from our real self, too ensnared in our false persona, we become depressed, and life seems meaningless.

This lack of meaning has been one of the major themes of the past century for philosophers, artists, and psychologists. When we direct our focus inward, however, we discover that we are not the "hollow men" that the poet T. S. Eliot described, but full of the natural power, love, and intelligence of our true nature.

Disentanglement and Spontaneity

As we recognize ourselves as the stillness of spiritual oneness, all of our experience flows freely through us. Each moment of life registers with its full impact. In this way, we become disentangled from the flow of life as we become more immersed in life. This is our most natural, relaxed condition. It is important that we do not try to hold our focus on either the stillness or the movement. To live in the dimension of spiritual oneness means that we do not hold onto any aspect of experience.

It is particularly challenging to allow life to flow in our intimate relationships, for it means that we cannot secure the source of our pleasure. The more we love someone, the more we may fear the changes that the dynamic flow of life might bring. But when partners can allow the true progression of change and growth in a relationship, they support each other in becoming real. In this way, they come to know themselves and each other with genuine intimacy.

One of the most important concepts of Asian religion is that all forms in creation are finite and temporal, coming together out of the favorable conditions of the moment and dissolving when those conditions no longer exist. To live with awareness of one's own mortality brings life into the immediate, vivid present. To understand that one's relationship with another person is also mortal brings the same sense of presence, actuality, and value to each encounter. It teaches us to hold the relationship gently, as a finite shape in life's ceaseless flow of circumstances, living out its true momentum in space and time.

Some people are afraid that to let go of their grip on themselves means that they will act on every destructive or lewd impulse that occurs in them. But fundamental consciousness is our dimension of wholeness. Although we do register all of our impulses in this dimension, our actions emerge from our whole being, including our mental clarity and compassion.

This awakening of spontaneity can be one of the most challenging aspects of spiritual realization. It may remind us of painful situations in our childhood when our hearts and minds were open and available while the adults with whom we interacted were far more guarded. To allow ourselves to become truly responsive and authentic again in a world that does not always return or honor those qualities requires courage. We can base this courage on compassion for the confusion and suffering that is shared, in various degrees, by all human beings.

It is also important to know that our true self, our spiritual essence, cannot be altered in any way. We can trust the absolute durability of our true nature. A Tibetan Buddhist teacher once told me that our true nature is "harder than a rock." In the Hindu literature, it is said to be "uncreated, unborn," and Zen Buddhism describes it as "I have never moved from the beginning."

Since fundamental consciousness is unchanged by the content of experience, it cannot be damaged. Although we can certainly feel emotional pain, our experience of essence is unchanged by it. Although we may feel that we have been severely damaged by circumstances in our past, once we reach the essence of ourselves, we know that we are essentially whole and well. None of our innate functions—our creativity or our capacity to love or think or experience sexual pleasure, to name just a few—can be diminished by another person. We can only constrict our own attunement to these indestructible aspects of our own being.

The ability to relax and allow ourselves to be as we are in each moment also means that we can allow other people to be just as they are. One of the major challenges of intimate relationships is accepting the "otherness" of another person. Many people protect themselves against the otherness of other people, because they fear that it will impinge on their own identity, that it will invade and curtail their own connection with themselves. But in the all-pervasive space of fundamental consciousness, there is plenty of room for one's own being and the being of another person. As we begin to live in this dimension, our inward attunement is no longer challenged by the otherness of another person. In the unchanging relational field of emptiness and presence, we can experience the movement of another person's experience at the same time as we experience the movement of our own experience. We can then observe, with interest and curiosity, how the exchange between ourselves and another person unfolds. This means that we are able to truly get to know that person and to interact with them. We don't have to make the relationship happen; we don't have to make it work in any particular way, for we see that the actual exchange between ourselves and another person unfolds to produce its own true form.

Exercises

The following three exercises can help you attune to fundamental consciousness, alone and with a partner. Fundamental consciousness pervades your individual form and everything around you in unity. The first exercise is about attuning to fundamental consciousness as it pervades your individual body. This is done by inhabiting your body—first part by part and then all at once. Inhabiting the body is different from being aware of your body. It means that you are actually present within your body. It feels as if you *are* the internal space of your body.

Everywhere that you inhabit your body, you are conscious. When you inhabit your whole body at once, you reach the subtle, unified dimension of fundamental consciousness.

This consciousness can be realized in the individual body by attuning to the quality of self. As I have said, this quality is an entranceway into our basic wholeness. Even attuning to the quality of self in one part of your body can help you experience the internal space of your body as a whole.

Fundamental consciousness is also achieved in this exercise by attuning to balance, such as the balance of the space in both your knees or both your hip sockets. The dimension of fundamental consciousness is absolutely still because it is balanced. Once you can experience this stillness as the ground of your being, as who you are, you can allow all of the movement of life, such as your thoughts, emotions, and sensations, to flow without obstruction. One of the ways to practice this in exercise 1 is to experience the stillness of the space and the movement of your breath at the same time. These are two different aspects of yourself, experienced together. Your consciousness is still and your breath is moving. The breath moves through the stillness of fundamental consciousness without disturbing or altering its stillness. With practice, you will be able to allow the movement of your thoughts, emotions, and sensations to flow through the stillness without disturbing the stillness. This means that you can allow life to occur in all of its intensity without being shaken from your realization of fundamental consciousness.

In exercise 2, you attune to fundamental consciousness pervading your body and environment at the same time. In this exercise, the oneness of fundamental consciousness pervades and transcends your individual form. However, your realization of this transcendent space is based on and requires that you inhabit the internal space of your whole body. In this way, your experience of individual wholeness (your inward contact with yourself) develops at the same time as your experience of oneness with everything around you.

As fundamental consciousness, all of the movement of life—including everything that you see and hear around you and even your own actions—flows through the stillness without disturbing your attunement to it.

In exercise 3, you attune to fundamental consciousness with a partner. You and your partner will be able to experience that you are made of the same unified field of sentient space, which pervades you both. You will be able to experience oneness with each other, while still inhabiting your own bodies.

These exercises are very effective "stretches" that can help you eventually settle into this dimension without effort. For best results, they should be followed by a short period of sitting meditation without any object of focus.

The exercises are designed to evoke subtle experiences that may be unfamiliar to you. If the instructions seem difficult to understand, allow yourself to respond to them without questioning their meaning. With practice, the intended experience will become clear, and understanding will follow from experience. You may find it helpful to tape yourself reading the exercise so that you can practice it without looking at the book. Partners can also take turns reading the instructions to each other.

EXERCISE 1 INHABITING YOUR BODY

Sit with your back straight, either on a chair or cross-legged on a cushion. Close your eyes. Breathe smoothly and evenly through your nose throughout the whole exercise.

Bring your attention down to your feet. Feel that you are inside your feet, that you inhabit your feet. Now attune to the quality of your self, a particular quality that feels like your self, inside your feet. (Make sure that you can stay in your feet as you breathe, and that your inhale does not lift you up out of your feet.)

Feel that you are inside your ankles and your lower legs. Attune to the quality of your self inside your ankles and your lower legs.

Feel that you are inside your knees. Now balance your awareness of the space inside your right and left knees; find both these internal areas at the same time. Experience the absolute stillness of your balanced consciousness. Feel that you are inside your thighs. Attune to the quality of your self inside your thighs.

Feel that you are inside your hip sockets. From the inside of your hip sockets, you can feel the internal space of your thighs and the internal space of your lower torso at the same time.

Balance your awareness of the space inside your hip sockets; find the inside of both hip sockets at the same time. Experience the stillness of your balanced consciousness and the movement of your breath at the same time. Feel that you are inside your pelvis. Attune to the quality of your self inside your pelvis. Bring your breath down into your pelvis on your inhale and let it pass through the quality of your self inside your pelvis.

Feel that you are inside your midsection, between your ribs and your pelvis, including the solar plexus area under the ribs. Attune to the quality of your self inside your midsection. Bring your breath down into your midsection and let it pass through the quality of self inside your midsection.

Feel that you are inside your chest. Attune to the quality of your self inside your chest. Bring your breath down into your chest and let it pass through the quality of self inside your chest.

Feel that you are inside your shoulders. Attune to the quality of your self inside your shoulders.

Feel that you are inside your shoulder sockets. From the inside of your shoulder sockets, you can feel the internal space of your upper arms and the internal space of your upper torso at the same time.

Balance your awareness of the inside of your shoulder sockets; find the inside of both shoulder sockets at the same time. Feel the stillness of your balanced consciousness and the movement of your breath at the same time. The breath passes through the stillness of your consciousness without disturbing the stillness.

Feel that you are inside your arms, wrists, and hands, all the way to your fingertips. Attune to the quality of your self inside your arms, wrists, and hands.

Feel that you are inside your neck. Attune to the quality of your self inside your neck. Bring your breath down through your neck and let it pass through the quality of self inside your neck.

Feel that you are inside your head. Feel that you are behind your whole forehead, inside your eyes, behind your cheekbones, inside your nose, mouth, jaw, and chin. Keep breathing as you do this. Feel that you are inside your ears. Now feel that you are inside both hemispheres of your brain. Feel the quality of your self inside your whole brain. Let your breath be subtle enough to move through your head and let it pass through the quality of self inside your whole brain.

Now feel that you are inside your whole body all at once. If we say that the body is the temple, then you are sitting inside the temple, with nothing left out. You are filling the internal space of your body with yourself. Attune to the quality of your self in your whole body. Keep breathing smoothly through your nose as you do this. Let yourself feel that you are made of the quality of self, all the way through your whole body.

EXERCISE 2 ATTUNEMENT TO INNER AND OUTER SPACE AS FUNDAMENTAL CONSCIOUSNESS

Begin at the end of exercise 1—with the breath moving smoothly through your body. Sit upright with your eyes closed. Feel that you are inside your whole body at once. Attune to the quality of self in your whole body. Keeping your eyes closed, mentally find the space outside your body, the space in the room.

Experience that the space inside your body and the space outside your body is the same, continuous space; it pervades you. You are still inside your body, but your body is pervaded by space.

Now open your eyes and again feel that you are inside your whole body all at once. Even though the world appears around you, you still have your own temple to sit within. Attune to the quality of self in your whole body. Mentally find the space outside your body. Feel that the space inside and outside of your body is the same, continuous space. It pervades you. This present moment is inside and outside you at the same time.

Experience that the space pervading your body also pervades the other people and objects in the room. But you are still inside your whole body. Do not project yourself into the other people or objects in the room. You are attuning to the space that is already pervading you and them.

Experience that the space pervading your body also pervades the walls of the room. Remain inside your whole body while you experience the space pervading both your body and the walls of the room. Now let go of any action of attunement and rest in the pervasive space of fundamental consciousness.

EXERCISE 3 ATTUNEMENT TO FUNDAMENTAL CONSCIOUSNESS WITH A PARTNER

Both partners should follow these instructions at the same time. Find a quiet place and a time when you will not be interrupted. Sit upright on a chair, facing your partner. Keep your eyes open. Breathe calmly and evenly through your nose. Experience that you are inside your whole body at once. Mentally find the space outside your body. Experience that the space inside and outside your body is the same continuous space.

Experience that the space pervading your own body also pervades your partner's body. Remain in your own body while you experience this. Do not project yourself into your partner's body. Attune to the space that is already pervading you and your partner. Let your breath pass through the space of your own body on both your inhale and your exhale (you are breathing your own location in space). Practice allowing yourself and your partner to just be in the space, continuous with each other but not merged.

Let your eyes relax. Your eyes are also pervaded by space; they are made of space. Experience that you are seeing each other with the space itself—the space does the seeing. The space sees both you and your partner at the same time. Let go of any action of attunement and rest in the pervasive space of fundamental consciousness.

If you do not have a partner, you can practice this exercise in any group of people—for example, in a restaurant or a theater. Experience that the space that pervades your own body also pervades the other people. Remain inside your own body as you do this, and let your breath pass through the space inside your own body. Practice allowing yourself and the other people to be just as they are, in the space.

II

ONENESS *and* SEPARATENESS
Overcoming Boundary Problems

All duality comes from the differentiation of a single ground.
THE PEARL GARDEN,
DZOGCHEN TANTRA

WHEN CHARLES AND MIRIAM came to work with me, they had been married for a year and a half. Although they were having difficulty adjusting to living together, the love between them was obvious. If either of them became upset while speaking, the other would watch with anguish and then reach over to pat and caress. When the first session was over, they handled the details of payment and setting the next appointment with a cozy, secure camaraderie. So I was almost as shocked as Charles when Miriam announced, during their second session, that she had decided to get her own apartment.

"I used to read books," she said, gesturing toward my bookcases. "I could think! My favorite activity was sitting with a book on philosophy or psychology and making notes in my journal. Now my favorite activity is lying in our bedroom in front of the TV with Charlie, eating nachos."

"You don't have to do that," Charles protested. "I can watch TV by myself, and you could go think in the living room."

"No, I can't," she answered. "There are plenty of afternoons when I get home and you're still at work. But I just don't get any thoughts anymore." She turned to me. "It's like I don't exist the way I used to. All I can feel is Charlie."

As she began to cry, Charles moved toward her and put his arm around her shoulders. Miriam leaned her head against his chest, and a strange thing happened. Her strength seemed to drain out of her; her intelligent presence became dim and diffuse. Still leaning against him, she turned her face to me and smiled weakly, and it was really as if she no longer existed; some vital part of her being had departed.

The Boundary Problem in Relationships

One of the most common problems that people have in intimate relationships is that they feel lost or submerged in the other person, or they fear that this will happen if they allow themselves to be truly intimate. Some people cope with this fear by distancing themselves from other people, by closing themselves off to external influence, or by finding ways to push people away. Others cope in a seemingly opposite way, by attempting to merge with the identity of their partner. Most of us do some of both. These relational styles are ways of accommodating the defensive barrier that we have created, early in our lives, between ourselves and other people. They are a continuation of the delicate negotiation, which begins in infancy and can last our whole lives, between connection with ourselves and connection with other people. This quandary of choice between self-love and love for others is, at root, illusory—for we are fundamentally whole within our own being and one with other people at the same time. Love is an essential quality of the whole field.

The fear of losing one's own identity in relationships is so central to the challenge of being intimate with another person that I could find some expression of it in all of the couples who come to work with me. To some extent, the fear of identity loss is the fear of ego loss. In an intimate relationship, our ideas about ourselves and our strategies for getting approval, maintaining oneupmanship, and so forth are always challenged. There is almost always some conflict between our partner's intimate view of ourselves and the image that we hold of ourselves. These conflicts can be very helpful for dismantling our holding patterns. But I have found that the reason so many people are unable to surrender their defenses in relationships is that they are defending something even more precious to them than their constructed ego. They are protecting their actual connection with themselves—their self-enjoyment.

Since the experience of self-connection is difficult to define, the loss of it is often expressed as a vague but intolerable malaise. It is described as a loss of "space," a sense of being "out of sync" with oneself. People may speak of feeling cut off from their own needs and desires or from their own thoughts and feelings. Some people feel as if they are seeing the world through their partner's eyes, that they can no longer connect with their own perceptions and responses. The loss of self-connection is experienced as a breach of boundaries, an inability to juggle the guarding of one's own perimeters with the openness of intimacy. The perceived threat of intrusion often gives rise to power struggles, turning the act of mutual decision-making into fight-to-the-death warfare.

The loss of self-connection is the inability to attune inward to the source of our own experience, within the internal space of our body. Our awareness of our partner overwhelms and replaces our contact with ourselves. But instead of feeling a connection with that person, we feel bound up in them.

In my last book, *The Enlightenment Process,* I quote R. D. Laing's description of the loss of self-connection. He writes, "If the individual does not feel himself to be autonomous this means that he can experience neither his separateness from, nor his relatedness to, the other in the usual way. A lack of sense of autonomy implies that one feels one's being bound up in the other, or that the other is bound up in oneself, in a sense that transgresses the actual possibilities within the structure of human relatedness. It means that a feeling that one is in a position of ontological dependency on the other (i.e., dependent on the other for one's very being) is substituted for a sense of relatedness and attachment to him based on genuine mutuality."[1]

This common difficulty in relationships can be particularly confusing and troublesome for people who are interested in spiritual transformation. Since spiritual realization is the unity of oneself and everything else, they ask, shouldn't we surrender our connection with ourselves? And isn't the resentment that one feels at being overwhelmed by another person's presence simply one's own clinging to the illusion of existing separately from that person?

In order to progress on the spiritual path, it is important to understand the difference between lack of self-contact and the dissolution of ego. In order to realize true oneness with other people, we need to recognize the difference between spiritual unity and the experience of being "bound up" in another person that R. D. Laing describes.

The Equality of Fundamental Consciousness

As I described in the last chapter, we experience the unified spiritual dimension of life as vast space pervading all of the various forms of life equally. This experience is sometimes called "nonduality" or "one taste." This unified existence is not something outside of ourselves. It includes ourselves. Our own being is the same one taste as everything around us. This is our most relaxed state.

As we let go of our defensive holding patterns, we can relax into the unified dimension of existence. This feels as if we are dissolving in space, becoming more and more permeable or transparent. At the same time, it feels as if we are truly existing, as if we are being born. It feels as if we are coming into contact with parts of ourselves, actual places within our body, that have been numb and unavailable, as if we are becoming whole within the internal space of our body. This is an emptiness of defensive structures and a fullness of our essential being. Spiritual oneness is not an experience of submerging our own existence in the existence of another person. It is not a diffusion of our own sense of being outward into the environment. It is a deepened and simultaneous contact with ourselves and our environment.

As I touched on in the previous chapter, spiritual oneness is not a return to the predefended condition of infancy. According to the observations of developmental psychologists, we begin life with just a rudimentary ability for self-contact and connection with other people. Early childhood development is described as the increasing ability to differentiate between ourselves and our environment, to recognize and express our own needs and perceptions, and, at the same time, as an increasing ability to connect with other people. Although children are as unguarded as spiritually realized adults, they have just begun the process of inward contact and connection with others that becomes fully developed with spiritual maturity.

A Model of Human Development

In the past two decades, psychologists have emphasized that childhood development always occurs in relationship with other people.

From the beginning of our lives, we exist in a relational field with our environment. The child's initial inward contact may come to fruition as the internal wholeness of spiritual realization. And the child's initial connection with the environment may mature into the spiritual oneness, the absolute unity of self and other. It is a process of growing toward inward and outward contact at the same time. Thus, the realization of spiritual oneness is a continuation of the child's budding experience of the self/other relational field.

As I described in the last chapter, letting go of our defensive structure is an important aspect of spiritual realization. But it is not the whole story. The letting go, or dissolving, of defensive structures only allows the process of human development to continue. The actual process of development is still a mystery, and it appears to be innate—a natural function. There appears to be a spontaneous movement toward increasing contact with the self and the other, or with the relational field as a whole, that drives the child's process of development and that continues to unfold in adulthood as we let go of our defensive grip on ourselves. Just as a tree needs the appropriate environmental circumstances to grow from its seed, human beings need the appropriate circumstances for this developmental process. But just as the tree and all of its basic characteristics can be predicted from the seed, spiritual realization, having the same basic characteristics universally, is the predictable outcome of human development.

The movement of human development proceeds through deeper levels of contact with ourselves and our environment. This deepening contact bring us into increasingly subtle and unified realms of existence or increasingly subtle attunement to ourselves and the world around us. This process arrives finally at the spiritual dimension of unified, fundamental consciousness, but there is still much further to go. When we reach the experience of "one taste," we have just begun the most advanced phase of human development. As I will explain more fully in a later chapter, we can continue to "fill out" our realization of spiritual oneness for the rest of our lives.

Suffering as a Schism in the Field of Oneness

According to developmental psychologists such as Margaret Mahler and Daniel Stern, children gradually deepen their connection with themselves as individuals, distinct from their environment. Mahler claims that we begin life in a state of merged identity with our primary caregiver and then proceed through what she calls the "separation-individuation sequence."[2] Stern says there is always some amount of self-distinction, even in infants, but that this increases over time. He also says that this deepening self-connection occurs simultaneously with the ability to connect with other people.[3] But both agree that the direction of childhood development is toward the recognition of self and other.

I describe this developing recognition of self and other as "spatial," as involving a shift in our experience of space, because it produces a deepening of perspective on life. At first, we can barely distinguish our own self from the people who hold and nurture us. Then we begin to discover our own sensations, emotions, perceptions, and needs as belonging to our own being. At the same time, we begin to recognize, respond to, and communicate with people who are other than our own being. This is a deepening of perspective, an increasing polarization of self and other.

When someone holds us, for example, we can sense that our own body is separate from their body. We begin to notice that the emotions of other people are different from our own and that we can feel sad, for example, as someone else feels happy or angry. As we continue to increase our experience of ourselves, we also begin to have an understanding of what is going on around us, and we form opinions, ideas, and beliefs around those events. Through the use of our developing verbal ability, we learn that our thoughts differ from those of other people; agreement and argument become possible. We become increasingly separate from other people, but because we are separate, we are able to touch them, to feel love and other emotions for them, and to communicate verbally with them. Inward contact gives us distance from our surroundings. At the same time, it develops our relational capacities, such as understanding, emotion, and physical sensation.

We reach our deepest perspective when we contact the subtle core of our body. This is a channel that runs vertically through the center of our body. It is our innermost connection with our own being. At the same time, it is our entranceway into fundamental consciousness, the dimension of our oneness with everything around us. In this way, our perspective—our sense of distance from our environment—develops simultaneously with our realization of oneness with our environment.

Thus, human development continues to unfold, under favorable conditions, toward spiritual maturity. But as it turns out, this process is so fraught with difficulty and obstruction that it tends to become arrested, or, at best, limited, in virtually every human life. By limited I mean that some aspects of ourselves become developed and others do not. Because the process of deepening self-contact and connection with others is not accomplished in isolation but in relationship with other people, it is greatly influenced by the capacity of those other people for self-contact and connection. In other words, it is difficult for us, as children, to become more distinct from our parents than they are from us or to be more connected with our parents than they are with us. The process of developing contact with both ourselves and others must accommodate our specific family legacy of developmental arrest and economy.

For example, in attempting to both separate from and connect with our mother, we will have to accommodate her own history of loss, abandonment, or rejection; her fear of connection or her anger at separation; her defenses that limit the depth of her sensation, love, and awareness, as well as her unconscious strategies for avoiding pain. And all of this accommodation and adjustment will occur in a complex economy in which some types of connection (emotional, physical, or mental) are available while others are obstructed.

As we navigate this relationship, we will both imitate her defenses and strategies and form our own. We will learn just how much and what kind of contact we can have with ourselves without loss of her love and just how much and what kind of connection we can have with her without loss of ourselves. We will make some compromises, trading a bit of self-contact for the sake of connection with her—or at least some semblance of connection, for true connection with others requires self-contact. We will also endure a degree of alienation from her for the sake of contact with our own sensations, feelings, and thoughts. But again, the contact we have with ourselves will be limited by our defense against connection with her, for all our defenses limit the relational field as a whole. Our defenses limit our self-contact and our connection with others equally. We cannot close our heart to someone else without closing our heart to ourselves. And this same complex navigation takes place with our father and other primary members of our child environment.

The constraints, attitudes, and strategies that we develop for both protecting our self-contact and for assuring our connection with other people harden with repeated use into habitual ways of being. In this way, our pattern of openness and defense, our degree of authenticity and distortion, our ability to trust the flow of exchange between ourselves and others or our need to manipulate it are all formed in relationship to the people we first encounter in our lives. Likewise, our ability to enjoy solitude, to notice our true desires and needs, to create, or to think for ourselves is formed within the context of these relationships.

Some of the defensive holding patterns that we form in these relationships become bound in the physical tissues of our body, constricting even our physical form. Other patterns emerge in response to circumstances that remind us of difficult situations in our past. All of these formations diminish the functions and capacities of our being. For example, with our own protective grip on ourselves, we limit our capacity for love and sensation. We constrict our senses. We restrain our voice and our creativity. We pull away from the support of the ground. We grip the muscles that we need in order to reach out or embrace or to take in nourishment.

These rigidities hold us in the perspective and economy of our childhood relational field. It is this defended relational field that we bring to our present relationships. Within the limitations of this field, we continue to negotiate the boundaries of self and other, and to balance self-contact with connection to others. In each new relationship, we confront the same riddle of how open we can be with this person without loss of our own self, and to what extent we can be who we really are without loss of their love.

Merging and Distancing

Our defensive patterns both contract and fragment the relational field. They form a defensive barrier between ourselves and our environment. At the same time, they hold us in our childhood perspective on life—in our childhood sphere of self and other. They hold us in the unresolved conflicts of our childhood, in the limitations of contact and the arrested flow of unexpressed responses. The defenses that were meant to protect us from the world actually keep us bound up in it, unable to get the distance (the inward contact) that we need in order to connect with other people.

In this contracted, fragmented relational field, we feel both too close to other people and alienated from them at the same time. We feel encroached upon, yet at the same time we feel unable to truly connect. We cope with this predicament both by distancing ourselves from others and by attempting to merge with them.

These two relational styles are not just sets of behaviors; they involve the placement of our attention in the relational field. People who mainly distance themselves from other people have trained their attention on themselves and attempted to ignore, or at least filter, the vivid presence of others. Because their defenses prevent them from actual contact with their own being, they seem to reside mostly in their thinking minds or their imagination, which sometimes gives them an air of abstraction or preoccupation. These people actually seem distant, as if they have a moat around them. But they are not really distant. They usually feel that life impinges on them with devastating force and that they must defend against it at all cost. To the best of their abilities, they are protecting their precious contact with themselves.

People who abandon their self-contact for the sake of connection place their attention more on other people than on themselves. When we relate with a person who is merging, we feel that they are too close to us, that they are in our "space." People who merge with others usually think of themselves as being very loving, very concerned for other people. And they have made a great sacrifice in order to feel connected with people. But because their inward contact is diminished, they cannot truly make the connection that they seek.

So both of these strategies for coping with the defended boundary between ourselves and other people are ineffective and unsatisfying. The self that we defend in isolation is just a shadow of our true self. And the connection that we make by attempting to merge with other people is just a fraction of our capacity for intimacy. It is through inward contact with our own organism that we become capable of true contact with other people. We grow toward our true distance from other people and our true oneness with them at the same time.

I first noticed this about thirty years ago, while I was living at a Zen monastery in upstate New York. It is an old joke that the hardest thing about being a monk is other monks, and although I was not technically a monk, this was particularly true for me. I arrived at the monastery at a very low point in my life. I had suffered some losses, of both my physical health and people close to me, several years before and had been living in near isolation ever since. I found the communal situations of monastic life almost unbearable, the boisterous presence of other souls bruising and disruptive. We were expected to eat all our meals together, to work together cleaning the monastery, and to socialize together on the two days each week when the formal schedule was suspended. We also meditated together twice a day, sitting in silence and absolute stillness, attending to our breath or to the compelling phrase of a Zen koan.

It was in this stillness that I first noticed the movement inward, how each breath brought me infinitesimally closer to the core of my body. As the year went by and this inward movement progressed, I began to notice that I felt further away from the people around me. I could look across the distance and connect with them. I could feel their presence while still feeling my own. I could also feel the stillness that was the same in all of us, that was continuous between us, and that was unchanged by even the most intense movement of thoughts, feelings, and sensations.

It is very interesting that when we inhabit the internal space of our body, the barrier between ourselves and other people dissolves. We experience oneness of our internal and external experience, a mutual transparency of self and other. But when we live on the surface of ourselves, as most people do, we live in divided space; we feel separate from everything around us. We can say that the world of the severely defended person is (almost) flat, whereas, at the other end of the spectrum, the world of the advanced spiritual master is (almost) round. This is a deepening of perspective, a deepening of contact with oneself and others.

How Two Hands Touch in Oneness

When we relate with another person in the dimension of spiritual oneness, we do not lose our essential identity. We experience that other people and ourselves are made of the same one essence without losing our own individual embodiment of essence. When we shake hands with another person in this dimension, we experience that our own hand is continuous with the hand of the other person. As fundamental consciousness, there is no separation between our own hand and the other person's hand. But at the same time, we know our own being in our own hand and the other person's being in the hand that we shake. The recognition of self and other is reflected in the clear, unified space of fundamental consciousness.

Whatever communication occurs between our own hand and the other person's hand is also clearly reflected in this space, in this unified relational field of consciousness within the two hands. One person may communicate love, for example, while the other communicates respect. The subtle currents of this communication move freely in the unobstructed space, producing a dance of intermingled currents, an excitement of interference patterns, that is transmitted throughout the energy systems of both people. And at the same time, as fundamental consciousness, we can each distinguish our own communication from the communication of the other person. This is the paradox of spiritual oneness: we are each whole within ourselves and unified with everything else at the same time.

Exercises

I always teach exercise 4 in the Realization Process teacher trainings, but it is an exercise that any two people can enjoy. In this exercise, you use physical touch to help each other inhabit your bodies. Feeling your partner's hands on your body can make it much easier for you to find and inhabit the internal space of your body. Their touch can help you experience the whole shape of each part of your body, in order for you to fill that shape with your own presence. It is also amazing to be the partner doing the touching. You can actually feel the other person become more alive between your hands as they inhabit their body. For many people, feeling that quality of aliveness in another person's body helps them to attune more clearly to that feeling in themselves.

Exercise 5 is about letting yourself receive another person's presence. Proximity to another person, even someone we love and want to be close to, often evokes unconscious defenses. These take the form of either closing ourselves off to the other person or vacating our own body so that we are not really there. But if you inhabit your body, you can receive the other person without feeling overwhelmed or in any way threatened by them. Your own presence within your body cannot be harmed; it is made of the unbreakable dimension of fundamental consciousness.

EXERCISE 4 HELPING YOUR
PARTNER INHABIT THE BODY

In this exercise, partners help each other contact and inhabit the internal space of the body.

Partner A sits upright on a chair.

Partner B stands behind the chair and puts his or her hands on either side of Partner A's head.

Partner A inhabits the space between Partner B's hands.

Partner B may be able to feel when Partner A inhabits the space between his or her hands. The space will feel alive with Partner A's presence.

Then repeat the exercise, changing roles.

This exercise can be practiced with any part of the body. For example, Partner B can put his or her hands on either side of Partner A's shoulder or leg or wrist, helping Partner A inhabit that internal space.

EXERCISE 5 RECEIVING EACH OTHER
IN THE RELATIONAL FIELD

Partners can practice this exercise either facing each other or sitting side by side.

Both partners follow the instructions at the same time.

Experience that you are inside your whole body at once. Find the space outside of your body, the space in the room. Experience that the space inside and outside of your body is the same continuous space, pervading you.

Experience that the space that pervades your body also pervades your partner. Stay in your own body as you experience this.

Now feel that you are inside your head—that you inhabit your head. Staying inside your head, open to your partner's presence and energy. Let yourself receive your partner's presence and energy within the space of your head. Be sure to remain inside your head as you practice this. Do not draw your partner's energy toward you, and do not project your own energy into your partner's head. Just inhabit your own head and receive your partner's energy and presence.

Repeat this exercise with your neck, chest, midsection, pelvis, and finally with your whole body at once.

III

DANCING
CORE-TO-CORE
Relating from the
Subtle Core of the Body

Kabir says: Tell me, what is God?
He is the breath inside the breath.

KABIR

Our Deepest Perspective

When we deepen our perspective from the periphery of ourselves to the innermost core of our being, we enter into fundamental consciousness. We come into unmistakable contact with the luminous, unchanging essence that pervades all forms in nature. This is not just a shift in the depth of our own being, but also in the depth of our relationship with everyone and everything that we encounter. The essential unity of ourselves and others is present in every situation. Even painful encounters are infused with the love and clarity of our spiritual essence. From the subtle core of our being, all of our relationships become intimate and spiritual.

It is often taught that fundamental consciousness has no center and no circumference. It is a vast, boundless consciousness that pervades all of nature evenly. When we live in this subtle dimension of life, we experience that our own being is a vast, open space that pervades everywhere. However, the teaching that fundamental consciousness has no center can be misleading, for in the human form there is an entranceway into fundamental consciousness that is, for each of us, its center. Connecting with this center, in the core of our being, is a direct and very effective way of realizing fundamental consciousness.

The entranceway into fundamental consciousness is a subtle channel that runs through the vertical core of the body from the center of the crown of our head and above to the center of the pubococcygeal muscle at the bottom of our torso and below. It has traditionally been described as a hair-thin straight line. When we contact it, we recognize it by its electric-like quality.

This channel is also our entranceway into our most subtle level of energy. We can view the human organism, and all other forms in nature, as having three dimensions: physical matter, energy, and consciousness. These are really three levels of attunement to ourselves. The energy system itself is quite complex; it is made of many different types and subtleties of movement. The breath is part of the energy system.

As we deepen our inward contact, we refine our attunement to ourselves. Then we realize that our breath moves everywhere in our body; it is part of a vast network of streaming movement and pulsation. We may also begin to see this subtle movement in the world around us, as light and vibration.

As we deepen our inward contact still further, we reach the subtle core of our body and the dimension of fundamental consciousness. At this point, we experience a more refined energy that moves through the subtle core of our body and branches out into our whole form. In the Hindu Yoga system, this energy is called *kundalini*. We experience our subtle core as an aliveness and fluidity in the innermost depth of our body. Contact with this energy feels as if something that has been rigid, unconscious, and unknown has been transformed into something both conscious and flowing.

The subtle core of the body is our deepest connection with our being. It is also our entranceway into oneness, our deepest and most subtle contact with everything around us. We arrive at our greatest distance from our environment and our oneness with our environment at the same time by penetrating into the subtle core of the body.

When two people connect with each other from the subtle cores of their bodies, they experience that fundamental consciousness pervades them both. They are each situated in the innermost depth of their own being and one with each other at the same time. This feels like a connection across distance. At the same time, it feels like the richest connection we can have with another human being. There is an automatic resonance between the two cores, a kind of "buzz." This feels like the pure essence of contact, like contact itself. It is something like the contact that occurs when two people hum the same note, except that the resonance occurs spontaneously—we do not create it—and it occurs in the core of our body.

Along with this resonance, there is a spontaneous flow of very subtle energy that moves between the two cores. This energy is a type of communication that can lead to a nonverbal understanding between partners. When two people relate with each other in the relational field of spiritual oneness, they experience that their relationship is made of both the unity and stillness of fundamental consciousness and the spontaneous exchange of subtle energy flow.

The Essential Qualities of Being

The subtle core of the body is the source of the essential qualities of our being. Fundamental consciousness is experienced as clear, luminous space—an unbroken emptiness that pervades all of our experience. Tibetan Buddhism describes this dimension as having the qualities of emptiness, clarity, and bliss. Hindu metaphysics describes it as having the qualities of being, intelligence, and bliss (Sanskrit: *sat chit ananda*). In the spiritual dimension, all of life is infused with emptiness or beingness, with a sentient luminosity, and with bliss. The more realized we become, the more vividly we experience these three qualities pervading ourselves and our environment. Fundamental consciousness appears to have no other attributes aside from these three.

However, just as clear sunlight contains the simultaneous spectrum of all possible colors, our spiritual essence can also be said to contain, or to be made of, all possible qualities of existence. This is so because there is absolutely no difference between our essential being and our spiritual dimension. The one self of fundamental consciousness is the same self that we have always known ourselves to be, only clearly experienced.

The spectrum of all our essential qualities is present in the subtle core of the human body. If we view the subtle core of the body from top to bottom, we can describe these qualities as awareness, emotion, and physical sensation. Awareness is entered into through the top third of the subtle core of the body, emotion through the mid-third, and physical sensation through the bottom third. The Hindu Yoga system delineates this spectrum still further into seven points along the core, called chakras, which are associated with subtle awareness, intuition, creativity, love, power, sexuality, and gender. The chakras are considered sensitive points where we can most easily penetrate the subtle core. We can "unravel" and release our complex knot of psychological defenses from the whole subtle core of the body.

Although everyone experiences physical sensation, emotion, and awareness, we reach the spiritual dimension of these qualities in the subtle core of our body. The spiritual dimension is a unity, an experience of all three qualities existing at once and pervading everywhere. It is an unchanging ground of awareness, emotion, and physical sensation, within which specific, constantly changing awarenesses, emotions, and sensations transpire.

The difference between what we might call ordinary awareness, emotion, and physical sensation and the spiritual dimension of these qualities is that in the spiritual dimension there is no separation between subject and object. For example, the same ground of awareness, emotion, and physical sensation that experiences the table in my room also experiences myself sitting next to the table. Another way to say this is that both the table and my own form are pervaded by (or made of) the same unbroken ground of awareness, emotion, and sensation. Yet a third way to say this is that the table and I both emerge simultaneously out of the same ground of awareness, emotion, and sensation. The table and myself are experienced as a whole.

Although we attune to each of these three qualities through specific parts of the spectrum, they all pervade everywhere as fundamental consciousness. In other words, we attune to awareness through the upper third of the subtle core, but the quality of awareness pervades our whole being and environment at the same time. We attune to the quality of emotion through the mid-third of our subtle core, but the quality of emotion pervades everywhere. The same is true for the quality of physical sensation, attuned to through the bottom third of the subtle core. Although it has not been spoken of much in the traditional religious teachings, the essence of physical sensation is an inseparable part of our individual wholeness and our spiritual oneness with all other life. The idea that we attune to the different qualities of being through one part of our body but that they each pervade everywhere is difficult to grasp intellectually. But, as you will see in the exercise at the end of the next chapter, it is not difficult to experience.

These essential qualities, entered through the subtle core of the body, make up the all-pervasive stillness of fundamental consciousness. They make up the ground of our experience, within which specific, changing sensations, emotions, and mental activities occur. When we reach the spiritual essence of these qualities, we become more open, more available for experience, and more deeply stimulated by life in all of these three aspects of ourselves. It is part of nature's mysterious design that even the most fundamental dimension of our being is made of this spectrum of qualities.

As fundamental consciousness, these qualities are not experienced as distinct from each other. Fundamental consciousness can be experienced as sheer transparency or as the quality-rich ground produced by the integration of these qualities.

Although fundamental consciousness is experienced as homogenous space, we can attune to these qualities in order to expand our realization of fundamental consciousness. This is important, because if we do not know about this spectrum of qualities, we tend to develop our spiritual realization only in that part of ourselves where we are most open (most in contact with ourselves) to begin with. For example, a mentally oriented person will automatically meditate in his or her head. This will cultivate the quality of awareness while emotion and sensation remain constricted. An emotionally oriented person will tend to focus on their heart in meditation, opening their emotional capacity even further, without addressing limitations in their awareness and physical sensation. This imbalanced development intensifies the psychological fragmentation that we each bring to our spiritual practice.

For example, Alex is a very intelligent friend of mine who has been meditating for over twenty years. He teaches philosophy in a university and is very articulate about his perceptions and ideas. But there is a distinct lack of engagement in the way he relates with people, which makes him seem remote and disembodied. His meditation has focused solely on developing the centers in his forehead and crown chakra. It is not that he was taught to meditate only in his head. But he was not given any instruction about his body at all, so he naturally spends his meditation sessions inhabiting the same part of himself that he inhabits in his life. For Alex, there has been, since childhood, a fragmentation between the pain that he carries in his heart and the excitement of his mental faculties. Although I do not think he has formulated this consciously to himself, my impression is that he conceives of spiritual realization as a golden nothingness that will someday encompass him and "blot out" the emotional pain in his life once and for all. But he cannot become free of this pain without opening his heart. By ignoring his heart in his meditation, he augments the pain that he is trying to escape.

Many traditional spiritual practices exacerbate this imbalance by instructing students to focus on only one area of themselves, such as their heart center. Many popular spiritual teachings today focus solely on the mentally oriented practice of "recognizing" nonduality. While this can be very helpful for stretching open the quality of awareness, it does not awaken the other aspects of fundamental consciousness. Over time, this imbalanced realization produces an uncomfortable predominance of experience in one area of our being.

Fundamental consciousness is a blend of awareness, emotion, and physical sensation. The capacity of our being for awareness, emotion, and sensation does not vanish as we realize ourselves as fundamental consciousness; rather, it deepens, unifies, and matures into its essence. We can access the subtle core of the body, and the integrated ground of our essential qualities, as we become free of psychological constrictions. Spiritual realization and personal development are therefore one and the same process. Even a yogi sitting alone in his or her cave comes into the fullness of being that develops with the realization of fundamental consciousness.

This process of spiritual realization also develops our ability to be intimate. Awareness, emotion, and physical sensation are not just the qualities of our individual being; they are also the qualities of oneness and the three major pathways of our exchange with other people. When we connect from the core of our own body to the core of someone else's body, we are in a spiritual relationship with them. We are able to relate to them from the most authentic and pristine source of our love, understanding, and sensation.

Penetrating the Subtle Core

It is difficult to make an exact correspondence between our physical anatomy and the subtle core of the body. It is sometimes described as the innermost core of our spinal cord, but the subtle core of the body is a straight line from top to bottom, while the spine is not. It has also been said that the subtle core of the body is in front of the spine—but we certainly cannot prove or disprove this. It is, however, most effective to focus inward toward the spine from the front of one's body.

We can best locate the subtle core of the body by the way it feels. This unmistakable electrical quality in the core, which I've mentioned, is our most trustworthy guide. There is also a sense of essence, or truth, in the core of the body that is difficult to convey in words but is easy to recognize when you come to it. In order to attune to this most subtle aspect of ourselves, it is necessary to make our focus extremely subtle and precise. This refined focus can penetrate into the subtle core.

In the Realization Process, we usually practice accessing the subtle core from three main points: the center of the head, the center of the chest, and the center of the pelvis.

The center of the head is located within the internal space of the head, between the ears. This point is sometimes taught as the sixth chakra in the Hindu system instead of the point between the brows. When we attune to the center of the head, we develop the awareness aspect of the fundamental consciousness that pervades all of our experience, both internal and external.

The heart center is exactly the same as the Hindu heart chakra. It is located in the center of the chest, deep in the subtle core of the body. Through this center, we develop the emotion aspect of fundamental consciousness. The more we open the knot of the heart center, the more the emotional ground of our being feels like pure love, or bliss. This blissful feeling pervades all of our experience even when we are experiencing a painful emotion like grief or anger.

The pelvic center is two or three finger widths below the navel, in the subtle core of the body. It is between the second and third chakras in the Hindu system. Through this center, we develop the physical sensation aspect of fundamental consciousness.

At the end of this chapter, there is an exercise for accessing one's own core and connecting with another person from each of these points. For everyone, there will be parts of the core that are more difficult to access than others. We each have our own pattern of psychological defense that blocks our inward contact with ourselves in particular parts of our body. We have to penetrate these rigidities in order to contact the core. This process often brings childhood feelings and memories to the surface. For example, people sometimes experience a release of grief as they contact their heart chakra. However, the more access we have to our core, the easier it becomes to recognize and release these holding patterns.

The Integrative Axis

The subtle core of the body is the integrative axis of our being. When we contact the core within our pelvis, chest, and head, we integrate the essential qualities of our being. This means that we can sense, feel, and understand at the same time. This integration is also the maturity, or the most subtle range, of all three essential qualities. As we begin to think, feel, and sense with our whole being, we become more capable of blissful emotion and sensation and original, intuitive thinking.

When two people relate to each other from all three points within the core of their bodies, it can help expand the range of their exchange with each other. When a couple is having difficulty communicating, it is often because each person is more open or in contact with different qualities of their being. For example, one person may live mostly in their awareness, while the other person lives mostly in their emotional capacity. This will influence both the manner and the content of each person's communication. And it will affect something more subtle, as I described above. There will be a lack of "resonance" between them that will make them feel mysteriously out of sync with each other. This imbalance can be resolved by connecting with each other "core-to-core" from the pelvis, chest, and head.

Last year, for example, a couple named Margaret and Carl came to see me. They had known each other only a few months and were on the point of splitting up. Although they enjoyed their sexual relationship very much and felt an unusually strong emotional connection, they had great difficulty communicating. They found conversation with each other difficult and even boring, and they had concluded that they were not really suited for each other. But because of the depth of their sexual and emotional connection they were unable to face the pain of losing each other. They both felt bewildered and trapped by the intensity of their bond.

During the first session, I taught them the exercise of contacting the subtle core of their own bodies within the three points of pelvis, chest, and head. They were both able to do this immediately.

I then gave them the exercise of connecting with each other from the subtle core of their bodies. They could connect with each other easily from the pelvis and chest points. When they connected from the subtle core of their chests (their heart chakras), there was an immediate and powerful resonance and a flow of love between them that both delighted and embarrassed them. But they were unable to feel the resonance of connection in their head centers. I thought this was interesting, because they had both been able to contact their head centers easily alone.

When I pointed this out to them, Margaret was able to explain the difficulty. She acknowledged to me, in a tone that suggested I would know exactly what she meant, that men did not appreciate a woman who was too mentally alert. As she was still in the "courtship" phase of her relationship with Carl and, in fact, had never been beyond that phase with any man, she said that she was making herself as attractive as possible by "dimming" her awareness.

Carl seemed genuinely shocked that Margaret would think he required her to be less intelligent than she was. We both encouraged her to take the chance of bringing all of herself to the relationship. We repeated the exercise, and this time they attuned at once to each other's quality of awareness. Then Carl began to cry. He had never before felt this mental intimacy with a woman. He said he felt "connected all the way through" with Margaret.

Throughout the following year, I watched this relationship grow into a friendship, an actual understanding of each other, that supported their love through all of the small crises that arose as they moved in together and planned for their future.

This exercise of connecting core-to-core is a very effective way to recognize the rigid subjective organization that each person brings to the relational field. Couples can experience for themselves where the exchange between them is blocked. The exercise also helps penetrate the defenses that are obstructing contact. As they continue to practice it, the couple will be able to unravel the complex skein of bound feelings, memories, and beliefs that produce the difficulties in their relationship.

Much has been written in the psychotherapy field about the way we form attachments to our parents. We may bond in a way that allows us to be sure of our parents' love even when they are not physically present, so that we joyfully welcome them when they return. Or, if our parents are unpredictable, often absent or neglectful, or abusive, we may bond in ways that reflect our ambivalence about our parents' love; for example, we may cling to our parents desperately or shut them out. These early attachment patterns affect the way we bond with people as adults. We may grow up doubting that love can really work, unsure that we are capable of loving or being loved. The exercise for partners to relate with each other core-to-core can help heal the energetic foundation of their bonds with each other, so that they can actually feel the exchange of love between them.

The Hindu Chakra System

The Hindu chakra system divides the continuum of physical sensation, emotion, and awareness into seven main points along the core. These are located at the base of the spine, in the sacral area, the navel area, the center of the chest, the base of the throat, the center of the head (or between the brows), and at the center of the top of the head. It is very helpful to focus on these points in order to expand one's realization of fundamental consciousness. Couples can also practice attuning to each other from each of these points. The chakra system is particularly useful for addressing specific problems in relationships.

About a year ago, a couple named Laura and Jack came to work with me as a last resort before ending their relationship. They had been together for five years and cared deeply for each other. They also shared a lively intellectual connection, and it was this that they most dreaded having to give up if their relationship ended. But neither was satisfied with their sexual intimacy. Jack felt that their sexual difficulties did not matter that much, but Laura said she missed having passion in her life and could not continue with Jack unless their sexual relationship improved.

When I taught them the exercise of attuning to each other from the three points along the core, they were able to experience the resonance between them in the center of the head and heart, but not in the pelvic center. Jack was unable to bring his focus deeply enough inside his pelvis to reach the subtle core of his body. I then asked them to direct their focus into the second chakra, in the area of the sacrum. This point is a little lower than the pelvic center, and it is associated specifically with sexuality.

As they attempted to contact each other from their second chakras, Jack said he felt that he was tightening up even more. By observing himself closely as he tightened against sexual contact with Laura, he realized that this movement of shutting down his sexual sensation was very familiar. As he continued to practice this exercise over the next few sessions, Jack remembered the injunctions against sexual feelings that he had learned in his family home. He had never been aware of his parents having any sexual feelings for each other, had never even seen them embrace. Gradually, he had tightened his own pelvis against his early stirrings of sexual feelings until it matched the tightness in his parent's bodies. As he brought his focus more deeply within his pelvis, he remembered several incidents in his childhood in which he had felt ashamed of his genitals. The worst was the time his mother had suddenly burst into his room as he was masturbating and threatened to tell their priest. With these insights, Jack was able to gradually release the tightness in his pelvis, and attune to the subtle core of his pelvis.

However, as Jack gained contact with his sexuality, Laura began to shut down. She found that she was afraid to feel contact with Jack from the core of her pelvis. We then entered another phase of work in which Laura remembered the frightening situations she had encountered when she reached puberty. There were groups of men in her neighborhood who would sit on the stoops in front of the old brownstones and make aggressive sexual remarks to the young girls who walked by. They made particular jokes about her breasts and would sometimes walk behind her while making loud kissing sounds. At home, she had to fend off the sexual innuendos and advances of her uncles. One of these men had finally forced her to have sex with him when Laura was still a virgin. All of her adult life, she had unconsciously chosen men who did not make any demands on her sexually. Gradually, with Jack's gentle support, Laura was able to overcome her fear and allow herself to feel sexual contact from her core to his. With practice, they added the sexual dimension to the love and intellectual contact they already shared.

Another chakra that is often important for couples is the third chakra, associated with power. This point is located on the level of the navel, in the core of the body. Many people have difficulty experiencing the essential quality of power. For women, this is usually because they have been taught that any display of power is unfeminine. Men often shut down their power early in life so as not to resemble male family members or cultural stereotypes whose power seemed brutal or dominating. So both men and women may grow up feeling powerless. When we feel powerless, we often attempt to protect ourselves from being overpowered by another person by weakening them in whatever way we can. This leads to the power struggles that challenge so many rela-tionships. The most effective resolution for power struggles is for both people involved to gain a true sense of their own power. By focusing within the third chakra, they can each develop power as an experienced quality in the body. When they connect with each other from their third chakras, they can experience the equality of true contact, rather than a struggle for dominance.

Although they do not appear on most charts of the chakras, there are several points above the head that can also be contacted. For couples interested in spiritual realization, it can be helpful to connect with each other from a point a few inches above the center of the top of the head. Again, this point can be located best by its electrical quality. If you cannot actually feel this point, you can begin by imagining a candle flame above your head. Just by keeping your focus on the space above your head, you will eventually become sensitive to the actual quality of the chakra. Any exercise of focusing on the space above one's head should be followed by "grounding" exercises, such as inhabiting the feet, legs, and pelvis, and focusing within the pelvic center in the core of the pelvis. Grounding is necessary so that your work with the upper part of the subtle core does not fragment you from the bottom of your body or from the energies that come up from the ground. In the Realization Process, we are cultivating wholeness, because fundamental consciousness is a dimension of wholeness—it pervades the whole body. If we open the top of ourselves but fragment ourselves from the ground, then we cannot attune to this most subtle dimension of ourselves.

It is important to understand that the practice of accessing one's core and connecting core-to-core with one's partner is just an exercise. We should be careful not to hold any position in ourselves. But as we continue to practice attuning to the subtle core of our body, we will find ourselves experiencing life from the perspective and integration of our core, without any effort. Couples will find that they gradually gain more continuity with each other. In other words, they both become more open to the dimension of spiritual oneness. This frees the flow of energy between them, and all of their communication becomes more authentic and spontaneous.

People often ask whether it is possible to relate core-to-core with people who are not attuned to the subtle core of their own bodies. Once we begin to live in the subtle core of our body as an ongoing experience, we do relate to everyone and everything we encounter from the core of our body. When we relate to someone who is not attuned to the core of their own body, we will not experience the same depth of contact that we feel with someone who is in the subtle core. This can be a valuable guide if we are searching for an intimate partner. We can experience whether a person is meeting us at the same depth that we know ourselves and whether the points of contact are sexual, emotional, or mental. This can also help us understand our relationships with other important people in our lives, such as relatives and coworkers.

If we have felt that someone—for example, a parent or a spouse— has not loved or understood us, it can be healing for our own psychological wounds to experience that person clearly from the subtle core of our body. Many sensitive people have grown up feeling unlovable and unrecognizable because the depth of their own feelings and awareness was not met by their family. They often describe a sense of being on the "wrong planet," of wishing that they could "call home" the way E.T. did in the movie. By relating with family members from the subtle core of our body, we may see that they simply did not have the inward contact with themselves that would have made them capable of the love and awareness we needed. This makes it easier to forgive both ourselves and them for the problems in the relationship. It enables us to stop waiting for them to finally recognize and love us, and to disentangle ourselves from the confines of that old relationship. This healing can even occur by imagining the person in front of us and relating to their image from the subtle core of our head, chest, and pelvis.

People often express the fear that they will be completely isolated if they live in the deeper perspective of their spiritual core. From my own experience and my observation of other people's lives, I have come to trust that if we are open to relationship, we will always find people with whom we can be truly intimate, whatever depth we grow to in ourselves. I have also found that living in the subtle core of the body helps us feel more kinship with people in general. We can see clearly the defenses that keep people from truly loving each other and recognize that they are similar to the defenses that we have encountered in ourselves. The subtle core of our body is our entranceway into the oneness of fundamental consciousness. Although there may be only a few individuals with whom we can enjoy core-to-core contact, we gain an ongoing sense of intimacy with life as a whole.

Disentangling from the Core

There are many ways to practice attuning to the points within the core of the body, which can facilitate spiritual realization. For example, it is helpful when you contact each of these points to feel that you are in the very center of the all-pervasive space of fundamental consciousness. You may be able to experience that the subtle core of the body opens out into fundamental consciousness, in all directions.

One of the most effective ways of working with the subtle core of the body is to absorb one's attention into it. Feel that you are living and breathing within the whole core. This absorption helps fill in the fragmentations in our contact with the core and stabilizes our realization of fundamental consciousness.

You can also practice letting go of yourself from (or as) the subtle core. As the subtle core of the body, we experience life without gripping or grasping at it. We allow life to be exactly as it is, to flow. As we unravel the knot of our being from the subtle core of the body, we can actually feel that we are disentangling from all of the content of our experience. We are becoming free. There is a sense that who we really are is literally letting go of whatever we are not.

The disentanglement of fundamental consciousness from the content of experience can help us feel less possessive in our relationships. As an exercise, the subtle core of the body can be used specifically for letting go of our entanglements with other people. You will find this exercise at the end of this chapter.

Not long ago, a woman named Gwendolyn came to work with me because she was suffering such severe depression that she was spending most of her time in bed. She was in her mid-seventies and had a successful career as a freelance book editor that was falling apart as she increasingly turned down work. She told me that her husband had died three years before. Although her friends all felt that it was time to end her mourning and "get on with her life," she did not feel capable of going on without him. They had been married for fifty-two years. As we spoke about her long marriage, I was struck by her lack of emotion. It turned out that although she had withdrawn from her life, she had not yet begun to mourn. She had barely cried since his death. She felt that if she allowed herself to grieve, she might get over the loss of him; she might really lose him.

I taught Gwendolyn the exercise of picturing her husband in front of her as she contacted each of the three points within the core of her body. I asked her to picture him as she inhaled and exhaled from within these points. At first, she found that as she inhaled, she pulled his image closer to her, and she worked with this for a while, pulling him in and pushing him away with her breath. Then I asked her to make her breath more subtle, so that it felt like she was breathing a mixture of breath and consciousness. Gwendolyn was amazed at how subtle she had to make her breath in order not to effect the image in front of her. Just as our entanglement with life is so subtle that most people never notice it, the process of disentanglement requires a very refined, precise inward attunement. With practice, she was able to feel less attached to the image of her husband. Although she could picture him vividly, she no longer felt that her own being was bound up with his. She was finally able to feel the pain of separation from him and to allow her tears to flow. This was the first step to regaining her vitality.

Exercises

Exercise 6 is based on one of the main exercises of the Realization Process, "the core breath." In this exercise, you find each of the points—the center of the head, chest, and pelvis—and you initiate the breath from within the points. This is an internal breath; both the inhale and exhale occur within the points. Air will still come in and out of your nostrils, but the first place you feel the breath move, on both the inhale and exhale, is within the core points. This subtle breath becomes integrated with the energy system. Each breath within the core points can be felt as a subtle resonance or vibration throughout your whole body at once.

Connecting with another person from the subtle core of the body can help you experience both the space of fundamental consciousness pervading you both and the interconnection of your two energy systems. You may feel an automatic flow of energy between you, as you find each other from the subtle core of your bodies.

The subtle core of the body is our entranceway into oneness with another person. In this dimension, we are both deeply connected with and disentangled from that person at the same time. We can love without grasping, without trying to pull that person closer to us or push them away. Exercise 7 shows how the core breath can be used to help you let go of a person who has become too entangled in your mind and heart.

EXERCISE 6 RELATING CORE-TO-CORE

Partners sit facing each other on chairs or cross-legged on cushions, with backs straight. Both partners follow the instructions together.

Close your eyes. Mentally locate a point in the center of your own head, between your ears. Look for the electric-like quality I've described to help you find it. Some people have described it as coming into a point of light within the relative darkness of the head. But it is important to experience this point, not to simply visualize it. Also, make sure that you are not too high in your head. You should be able to feel the bottom of your torso just by being in the center of your head (there is an automatic resonance down through the whole subtle core when you are in the center of your head).

Inhale by bringing the breath through your nostrils and into the center of your head. The breath comes in through both nostrils and then becomes a single stream of breath that can penetrate through your head to the center. Exhale through your nostrils.

Now *initiate* the breath from within the center of your head, as if there were air in the center of your head that you can breathe. The center of your head draws in the breath on the inhale, and releases the breath on the exhale. The breath will still enter and exit through your nostrils, but it will feel like the center of your head is inhaling and exhaling. It should feel as if the center of the head inhales a mixture of breath and consciousness, or as if the mind is breathing inside the center of your head.

Open your eyes and remain in the center of your head. Make eye contact with your partner across the distance between you.

Be aware of how much distance there is between you as you look at your partner. It will probably feel as if you become further away from your partner. This is your true distance from that person.

Find the center of your head again. *From the center of your own head,* mentally find the center of your partner's head. Be careful that you do not leave the center of your own head as you do this. You do not have to move at all to find the center of your partner's head. When you are able to do this, you will feel a resonance between the center of your head and your partner's head.

Close your eyes, and again mentally find the center of your own head. From the center of your head, find a point in the center of your chest, as deeply inward as you can bring your focus. You will recognize it by its electric-like quality. This is your heart center.

Now initiate your inhale from inside your heart center, as if there were air inside your heart center that you can breathe. It feels as if the heart center itself draws in the breath. Your exhale is a release from inside your heart center. As you practice this, let your breath become increasingly subtle and silent, until it feels as if the heart center draws in a mixture of breath and consciousness, or as if the mind is breathing inside the heart center.

Open your eyes and, staying in your heart center, make eye contact with your partner. Again, be aware of the distance between you as you make eye contact.

From your heart center, find the heart center of your partner. Be careful that you do not leave your heart center as you find the heart center of your partner. Try to trust that you will be able to connect with your partner from your core without coming out of yourself. There is a particular tendency in the heart center to project our love toward other people, if as to convince them that we really do love them. However, the projection of love is really less heartfelt than the core-to-core connection, because it separates us from the source of our love in our core.

Close your eyes, and again mentally find the center of your own head. From the center of your head, find a point about two inches below your navel, but as deeply inward as you can bring your focus. You will recognize it by its electric-like quality. This is your pelvic center.

Initiate your inhale from inside your pelvic center. It feels as if the pelvic center itself draws in the breath. Your exhale is a release from inside your pelvic center. Again, the breath will feel like a mixture of breath and consciousness, or as if the mind is breathing inside the pelvic center.

Open your eyes and, staying in your pelvic center, make eye contact with your partner. Be aware of the distance between you as you make eye contact. Now, from your pelvic center, find the pelvic center of your partner. Be careful that you do not leave your pelvic center as you find the pelvic center of your partner.

Close your eyes, and find the center of your own head. Now find the center of your head and your heart center at the same time. And then find all three centers at the same time: the center of your head, your heart center, and your pelvic center.

Initiate your breath from within all three centers at the same time. Your exhale is a release from within all three centers. Be patient with yourself; this will probably take a little practice. Feel that all three centers breathe a mixture of breath and consciousness, or that the mind is breathing in all three centers.

Stay in all three centers as you open your eyes and make eye contact with your partner. Be aware of the distance between you. Staying in all three centers in your own core, find all three centers in your partner's core. Stay in your own core as you do this.

EXERCISE 7 DISENTANGLING
FROM ANOTHER PERSON

Sit upright with your eyes closed. Feel that you are in your whole body at once. Picture in the space in front of you the person that you wish to disentangle from.

Feel where in your body you feel most attached to this person.

Find the subtle core of that part of your body. For example, if you feel most attached through your heart, you can find the point in the subtle core of your chest.

Continuing to picture the person in front of you, initiate your breath from within the core point. Both your inhale and exhale occur within the core point, as if there were air there that you could breathe.

Although this is an imaginal exercise, you may find that your grip on the image of the person is actual, that it involves an actual holding pattern in your breath and body. For example, you may find that your inhale pulls this person closer to you. Make your breath more and more subtle within the core of your body until it does not pull on the image at all.

Sit and breathe within the core of your body, allowing the image of the person to be in the space in front of you without affecting it with your breath. Now dissolve the image of the person. Feel that you inhabit your whole body at once—make deep contact with yourself. Sit a moment, breathing within the subtle core of your body.

IV

MUTUAL CONTACT
The True Meeting
of I and Thou

All fully awakened beings abide inseparably in the expanse
of Primordial Awareness, and all are in essence one.
JIG-ME LING-PA

ONCE WE HAVE AWAKENED to the spiritual dimension of ourselves, we live in an ongoing experience of unity, or inseparability,
with everything that we encounter. We live in a dimension of spaciousness and stillness that renders all experience fundamentally
equal. This "one taste" experience is also a dimension of luminosity and sweetness or, as we become more open, blissfulness. The
unity, brightness, and bliss of spiritual consciousness infuse all of
our relationships: with people, with nature, and even with inani-
mate things.

However, our relationships with the various things and beings
we encounter are also quite different. One important difference is
the degree of mutual contact that can be experienced. For example, someone who has realized fundamental consciousness can

make great contact with a table. First of all, they feel unified with the table; the clear-through empty space of spiritual consciousness pervades both the table and themselves. When they put their hand on the table, they can touch it all the way through its depth, so that they feel not only the texture of the table's surface but also the vibratory quality of the wood. They may even feel a flow of love from their own heart toward the table, for example, if the table has been in their life for many years. But the table itself has no discernible response, either to their touch or their love. It is a safe bet that the table is not even aware of this person in any way and certainly has no sense of blissful unity with them.

If the same person puts their hand on a living tree, however, they will feel some small response to their touch. Although I'm sure some would argue this point, many people who have spent time communing with nature will agree that the communing is not strictly a one-way affair; there is a small degree of mutuality to the contact. If this person puts their hand on an animal—a cat, for example—they will feel even more response to their touch. I'm not speaking about a response like purring or scratching, but rather a mutuality of the touch itself. We could describe this as a "touching back" from the cat to the person, but it is not a volitional activity. Rather it is an automatic, spontaneous result of the meeting of two conscious beings. This mutual touch between person and cat is not just a tactile experience. It involves the person's whole being and the cat's whole being. It is made of the essential qualities of being: awareness, emotion, and physical sensation.

There is more mutual contact with a cat than with a tree because a cat is more conscious than a tree. Contact is a function of consciousness. A cat is more conscious of its environment than a tree and probably more conscious of its internal experience as well. In the terms that I have been using in this book, the cat is more open than the tree to the relational field of self and other.

For this same reason, there is more potential for mutual contact with a human being than with a cat. This is not meant to minimize the depth of contact that we can feel with animals, especially with our own pets and with highly intelligent animals, such as dolphins.

Human beings are complex, so we can have different kinds of contact with different human beings, depending upon our respective organization of openness and defense in the aspects of awareness, emotion, and physical sensation. This organization is not entirely static; it shifts with the development of trust and other factors. But again, I am not speaking here of action or behavior. Mutual contact is an experience of spontaneous resonance that can occur with anyone who is open to life in the same ways that we are.

The greatest degree of mutual contact occurs between two people who have both realized fundamental consciousness. When we connect with another person in the oneness of the spiritual dimension, we recognize them by the depth and intensity of our mutual contact. Zen Buddhism says of this encounter, "Like two thieves in the night, they recognize each other at once."

When two people meet in the dimension of fundamental consciousness, they experience themselves as a continuity of awareness, love (or bliss), and physical sensation. As I described in the last chapter, the spiritual dimension of these three qualities is different from conventional experience. It does not only feel, for example, that one is aware of the other or that one loves or senses the other, although these aspects of relationship still occur. But there is also a fundamental experience that they are made of a single presence of awareness, love, and physical sensation. Contact is an inherent part of this continuity of presence. Fundamental consciousness pervades all life, and as fundamental consciousness, we experience contact with everything that we pervade. Also, the more we realize ourselves as the stillness of fundamental consciousness, the more fluidly and subtly our energy system flows. When two people are both attuned to this dimension, there is a spontaneous flow and exchange of energy between them.

Interestingly, contact does not require spatial proximity. As we become more open to life, we find that we have the ability to contact people at a distance. The first time I experienced this was in my early twenties. I had enrolled in a Silva Mind Control course to help me overcome my addiction to cigarettes. I don't remember the teacher's name, but I can still picture her vibrant face. On the last day of the three-day course, I overslept. I was awakened by a strange, unembodied "nudge" that I recognized at once as the presence of the teacher. She had managed to locate me, asleep in my bed, and to give me a wake-up call.

I met my husband thirty years ago while we were both living at a Zen monastery in upstate New York. Once, during a *sesshin,* a week of intensive meditation and silence, when we had known each other only a few months, we happened to pass each other in the hallway. Observing sesshin silence with our eyes focused on the ground, we paused to acknowledge each other. Suddenly there was a spontaneous resonance between us that lit our heads, then our hearts, then our pelvises, like three bells sounding.

The Qualities of Contact

We can divide, or categorize, the unity of our essential being in many different ways. For example, as mentioned earlier, the Tibetan Buddhists describe the spiritual dimension as having, or being made of, three qualities: emptiness, luminosity, and bliss. The Hindus say that it has the qualities of being, intelligence, and bliss. In the Realization Process, I divide it into essential awareness, emotion, and physical sensation. We can also divide the human organism into consciousness, energy, and matter or into the motionless ground of experience and the changing content of experience. These are all schematic divisions of something that is essentially indivisible.

In this chapter, we will look more deeply at the essential qualities of awareness, emotion, and physical sensation. Within the unchanging stillness of these essential qualities, we experience the movement of specific perceptions, cognitions, emotions, and sensations. (The subject of perception will be addressed separately in chapter 5.)

Awareness, emotion, and physical sensation are three modalities of experience, three arenas of openness to the spontaneous flow of life. They are also three aspects of our contact with other people. As we deepen all three qualities in ourselves, our responses to life and our contact with other people gain richness, complexity, and range.

One of the major principles of wholeness is that all of the "parts" contain all of the other parts. For example, the essential nature of our little finger is awareness, emotion, and physical sensation. We have the ability to attune to each of these qualities separately or to experience them as a unity. The purpose of attuning to each of the essential qualities separately is in order to recognize and release the defenses that specifically constrict each of them. As this release occurs, the fragmentations between these aspects of our being dissolve. As the fragmentations within our own being dissolve, the fragmentations between ourselves and other people also dissolve.

In the spiritual dimension of ourselves, we are free. This is not a freedom from life and it is a freedom of life. It means that our being itself is free and that our awareness, love, and sensation are available to receive and respond to life. The more we attune to fundamental consciousness, the more our thoughts, feelings, sensations, perceptions, and actions seem to emerge directly from the empty, all-pervasive space of fundamental consciousness.

Just as our essential qualities are actually an indivisible continuum, the body, in its undefended state, provides an integrated
unity of these three types of experience. There is, at root, no difference—no separation—between the physical body and the
most subtle dimension of consciousness. The essential nature of
the physical body is fundamental consciousness.

There is a direct correlation between where we are open or
defended in our body and our degree of attunement to the qualities of awareness, emotion, and physical sensation; however, all of
the qualities of our being pervade everywhere in our body. For
example, even though we need to be open in the upper third of
our body and to access the upper third of the subtle core of our
body in order to reach the essential quality of awareness, this quality pervades everywhere in our body. This means that as we realize
the spiritual dimension of ourselves, we are able to experience
awareness, emotion, and physical sensation everywhere within our
whole being.

This is easier to experience (see the exercise at the end of the
chapter) than to grasp intellectually. However, I think it can best
be understood in the light of the self-similarity theory of fractals.
Although that subject is beyond the scope of this book, I will
say briefly that according to self-similarity theory, each form in
nature is made of one pattern repeated throughout itself on different scales. A branch of a tree mirrors the form of the tree itself.
In this same way, the spectrum of awareness, emotion, and physical
sensation that makes up the whole body is also repeated in each of
the body's parts, no matter how small.

We can see the application of this principle in bodywork techniques such as foot reflexology, in which different parts of the body
can be energized by stimulating corresponding parts of the foot.
The correspondence is very simple: it is as if the general shape of
the body were imprinted on the foot. Rubbing the toes energizes

the top of the body and rubbing the heel energizes the bottom of the body. Interestingly, in the healing technique of Jin Shin Jyutsu, this same correspondence is used in the toes themselves: rubbing the tip of the toe energizes the top of the body and rubbing the bottom of the toes energizes the bottom of the body. In fact, any part of the body may be used in the same way. For example, the correspondence of the hands to the whole body is used for healing both in hand reflexology and Jin Shin Jyutsu.

For this reason, a defensive constriction in the head limits our awareness, and it also produces a constriction throughout our whole being. Likewise, releasing a constriction in our head will deepen our capacity for awareness and produce more openness throughout our whole being.

Along with specific holding patterns in each of the three aspects of experience—awareness, emotion, and physical sensation—we also create artificial fragmentations between them. We separate our awareness from our emotions, our emotions from our physical (and sexual) sensations, and so on. As we reach the spiritual dimension of ourselves, we are able to perceive, think, feel, and sense at the same time. Each moment of our lives registers as a unity of perception, cognition, emotion, and sensation. This enriches all of our interactions with other people. For example, our physical contact with other people is integrated with emotion and awareness. This enables us to have a more intimate relationship with another person.

Awareness

The essential quality of awareness is a wide-open mental clarity that pervades our whole body and environment at the same time. In religious terms, this experience is referred to as gnosis, an ongoing experience of knowing God. In relationships with other people, it is an ongoing mental connectedness, a sense of being of one and the same mind with everyone we encounter. This experience of unified awareness with other people persists even when we experience specific intellectual conflicts with them.

As we open to this aspect of fundamental consciousness, we gain the spontaneity of our mental faculties. We are available for the inspiration of our own unique thoughts. Original, spontaneous thought is the natural, essential function of the human mind. Although civilization always tends toward conformity, we can gradually free ourselves from the hypnotic influence that our family and culture have had on our minds.

To live in the essential quality of awareness also means to be receptive to the intellectual stimuli around us. Many sensitive people shut out the ideas and opinions of other people because they know how easily they lose track of their own inner voice. I knew one man who did not even read books because he feared the intrusion of other people's knowledge. But this defensive tactic had left him mulling over ideas that came to him many years ago in his youth, which were by now too familiar to excite him. Our awareness is an important aspect of the "open system" in which we grow. Awareness is also a vital part of our intimacy with other people. It can be as pleasurable to be mentally aroused by another person as it is to be moved emotionally and physically.

When we live in our essential awareness, we have our own unique understanding of life, our own perspective. This understanding is not static; it keeps developing. But it retains its unique identity, as characteristic of our individual being as the sound of our voice. We have all heard stories of saints and prophets receiving revelations from the spiritual dimension. But the process of spiritual development is revelatory for everyone. It is important to remain open to the unfolding of our own insight, not to drown it out with the static revelations of religious teachings or the generalized messages of commercially driven media. This is important for us collectively as well as personally. When we can hear and express our spontaneous thoughts, we help to bring truth into the world. Even if we do not relate with many people, we help our culture become more intelligent and authentic, and we help it progress in its understanding of reality.

It is sometimes taught that spiritual realization means having no thoughts. Many beginning meditation techniques are designed for emptying the mind. For example, there is a technique in Zen Buddhism in which the meditator attempts to count ten consecutive breaths, returning to the number one each time she has a thought. This usually winds up as a meditation on the number one. This technique can help us gradually eliminate the surface mental chatter or habitual "tape loops" that prevent us from settling into more subtle levels of consciousness. But the more advanced Buddhist teachings speak of a "non-abiding" mind, in which the movement of our thoughts flows through the stillness and emptiness of our being without disturbing or altering it in any way. In *Zen Mind, Beginner's Mind,* Zen master Shunryu Suzuki writes, "To stop your mind does not mean to stop the activities of mind. It means your mind pervades your whole body."[1] As we reach the all-pervasive dimension of consciousness, we realize that our awareness is an all-pervasive stillness. But within this stillness, our thoughts move freely and spontaneously.

Spiritual realization is also described as a lack of "mental elaboration" on our experience. This means that we do not project our past experience onto the present. We do not obscure our awareness of the present moment with preconceptions and fantasies. We live in what Zen calls "don't know mind." Some students of Buddhism interpret this phrase to mean a lack of cognition altogether, suggesting that spiritual realization means living in a world of perceptual stimuli without any cognitive recognition of these stimuli. But I believe this is a mistaken reading of the teaching.

"Don't know mind" is a cognition that is fresh in each moment, that is not limited by either repression or projection. It means that we allow each moment to arrive unanticipated and unmodified. A Tibetan Buddhist text describes the spiritual dimension as the "total field of events and *meanings*" (italics mine).[2] Another text calls it "the great empty cognizance."[3] It is the nature of essential awareness to know.

The essential quality of awareness is our ordinary awareness, clearly experienced. It is the most relaxed, natural condition of our awareness. In order to relax our awareness, we need to relax those parts of our physical body that are associated with mental activity. Most people have defensive holding patterns and habitual ways of being that produce constriction in their heads. One of the most common reasons that we constrict our awareness as children is to accommodate our parents' view of reality or the view of reality that our parents want us to have. For example, there may be a tacit family agreement not to notice the drunken behavior of a family member. Or our parents may fear that we will outwit them or in some way gain the upper hand, if we are allowed to have our own opinions. We may be told, either outright or through more subtle messages, that we are "too smart for our own good," or something of the sort. Because of these defensive patterns, and because of the ways we have mirrored the openness and defenses of our parents, and because of other, more mysterious factors like talent, we all use some aspects of our mental faculties more than others. This means that most of us inhabit and use some parts of our brain more than other parts. As we realize fundamental consciousness, we are able to inhabit our whole brain at once. Then our mental processes include the whole range of our mental abilities, including intuition and imagination. This greatly enhances both our understanding and our creativity.

Relaxing into the essential quality of awareness produces a profound change in the way we relate with the world. For example, I worked with a woman who grew up in an atmosphere of intense intellectual competition. Her father seemed capable of relating only on an intellectual level with his children, and his rare gestures of approval were always awarded for displays of mental ability. She remembered dinnertime as a battlefield of aggressively dazzling conversation. If she was not able to match or better her brother's demonstration of verbal prowess and knowledge, she would become the target of her father's disdainful humor. This was so painful for her that she would always come to the dinner table with a prepared presentation of some topic that she had selected from a magazine or newspaper. As an adult, she still felt it necessary to stand out intellectually in any social situation. Even for parties, she would prepare a topic of conversation that she could discuss articulately and in depth.

When I met her, she described a feeling of tightness, like a fist in her brain, that never went away. She also complained of feeling unreal, as if she were always pretending to be smarter than she really was. As she practiced attuning to the awareness aspect of fundamental consciousness, the tightness in her brain relaxed. After several months, she reported feeling that her mind was both "inside and all around her" but that it was "resting." She could feel her intelligence as an ongoing presence so that, for the first time in her life, she knew without doubt that she was not stupid. She described this constant presence as a "brightness and clarity without effort." She practiced going "as is" to parties, without a prepared speech. She found that she could sit there silently—in the beginning with studied concentration and then finally with ease—until something actually occurred to her to say. The spontaneity of her thoughts delighted her. "Sometimes I don't even say them out loud," she told me. "I just enjoy them myself." Without the pressure to perform competitively, she could take pleasure in her intelligence, as well as in the thoughts and ideas of the people around her.

The quality of awareness is often used as a path to spiritual realization. For example, some teachers say that we can achieve spiritual unity by being attentive to each moment. If we sit still and simply attend to each present moment, we will (very gradually) let go of our holding patterns and deepen toward the spiritual dimension. However, the most deeply ingrained defensive patterns will probably not succumb to this technique, or at least not for a very long while. It is also important to understand that all attention is not equal. Because of our deeply held defensive patterns, we may remain in a more superficial awareness of the present moment and not reach the very subtle awareness that is the spiritual dimension.

Some other methods of realizing essential awareness are attunement to the subtle core of the head, as I described in the last chapter, or attunement directly to the quality of awareness (as in the exercise at the end of this chapter). Some Zen koans also work on releasing the "awareness knot" by directing the full force of one's mental faculties to an unanswerable, mind-blowing riddle. All of these approaches are "stretches" for the quality of awareness. They can help deliver us, in increments, toward spiritual freedom.

It is important, however, to recognize that awareness is not the whole nature of spiritual oneness. Since our organism is a unity, we might conclude that stretching open the quality of awareness will open our whole being, and this is true to some extent. But our qualities of emotion and physical sensation are often so deeply (and unconsciously) constricted that opening only the quality of awareness actually intensifies our fragmentation. Also, because the rigid holding patterns in our body make it uncomfortable for us to inhabit our body, there is a common tendency for people to place their awareness in the world around them and ignore the internal space of the body. They may even feel that in doing this they are following the Buddhist teaching of the "nonexistence" of the separate self. But the spiritual "emptiness" of the self is a unity of self and environment, a unity of internal and external experience. It is always based on internal contact with our own individual form. Wherever we are in contact with the internal space of our body—wherever we inhabit our body—we become open to life. It is this openness of our own form that allows us to live in the unity of self and other.

Emotion

The essential quality of emotion is distinguishable from the qualities of awareness and physical sensation. As we become more attuned to this aspect of fundamental consciousness, we begin to experience it as sweetness or love. We experience an ongoing, unwavering, subtle quality of love pervading our body and our environment at the same time. This is unconditional and unconditioned love. It is not love for someone or something; it is love itself.

This unwavering love is not disturbed by the movement of our specific emotional responses. For example, we can experience a wave of sadness or a surge of fury moving through the ongoing quality of love in our body without disturbing it. In fact, our specific emotions become deeper and more spontaneous as we realize the essential quality of emotion. But they also become more appropriate to our actual circumstances—less triggered and less intensified by our projections of past events onto the present. Arising directly out of the essence of our being, our emotions are entirely fluid and transient. Whether or not we express them, they flow through us and dissipate without a trace.

No one reaches adulthood without some degree of emotional constriction. We defend ourselves against feeling emotional pain by arresting the energetic flow of our emotions. If this is repeated over time—or if the arrested emotional response is particularly intense—the muscular action required for the binding of the emotional response becomes a chronic pattern of tension in the body. The whole moment of response is caught in this arrested flow, so that our holding patterns contain both the memory of the painful event and the unspent energy of the emotional charge. In this way, we actually hold old grief, anger, and fear within our organism. These bound emotions color our present experience. For example, no matter how much we know of our childhood history, the grief held within our body will continue to make life seem sad to us as adults, until that arrested grief is allowed to flow and discharge.

We need to have released some degree of our bound emotional pain before we are able to realize fundamental consciousness. However, once we have realized the spiritual dimension, we can accelerate the process of emotional release. As fundamental consciousness, we are, in a sense, deeper than our emotional binding. By finding this subtle dimension within the binding, we can more easily unravel the held pattern.

For the past year I have worked with a man with a long history of depression and almost as long a history of psychotherapy. When I first met Paul, I thought of the phrase "sad sack" because he was so huddled into himself and deflated. He cried continuously as told me about his sad childhood, abandoned by both parents by age four, sent from foster homes to uncaring relatives and back to foster homes, having to start at a new school each time he moved. He cried as he told me about his failed therapies, years of psychoanalysis, of screaming and beating pillows, of regressive therapies, dream analysis, and antidepressants. Although he had no motivation to meditate on his own, at each of our sessions I led him through the exercise of attuning to the pervasive space of fundamental consciousness. He often complained to me about the futility of this exercise, saying that he felt no lasting change from it.

One day last month, Paul came in with a new complaint. He told me sadly that he could both see and feel a kind of thickness, like "thick water," in the space around his body. I asked him to direct his focus within the thickness and to attune to its emotional quality. He was able to do this without difficulty and reported that it felt like sadness. He said that he now realized that this sadness had always been there, as far back as he could remember, but that he had never actually seen it before. I then asked him to just observe the thick sadness in the space, as we sat silently together. After about twenty minutes, Paul began to cry. It was not the steady drizzle of tears that almost always accompanied his speech, but deep sobs that opened his whole throat, the outraged, desperate wail of an abandoned child.

Since that session, Paul has been able to meditate on his own. He reports that the space of fundamental consciousness is becoming increasingly clear and that he sometimes feels happiness in his body for no reason at all. Having visible, palpable evidence that sadness, although so familiar, is not really him but something that he has carried within himself, he has begun to take an interest in his own healing process.

The essential quality of emotion can be attuned to directly or by accessing the subtle core of the chest. It can also be opened through devotional prayer and through service to others. Self-love and love for others deepen simultaneously in the spiritual dimension. Like awareness, unconditional love is the essential nature of the whole relational field of self and other. It is the essential nature of both our internal contact with ourselves and our mutual contact with other people.

Physical Sensation

The essential quality of physical sensation is the aspect of fundamental consciousness that has been least mentioned in the traditional spiritual teachings. But physical sensation is an inseparable part of our own essential being and our oneness with other life. The realization of the essential quality of physical sensation is as necessary for spiritual maturity as the qualities of love and awareness.

Without the quality of physical sensation, our experience of the world lacks texture and tactile pleasure. Our intimacy with other people lacks sensual pleasure. And without this essential aspect of ourselves, our realization of fundamental consciousness is always fragmented. Our entire being is the instrument, or the vessel, of spiritual realization. If we keep part of this vessel closed, then we deprive ourselves of our full range of spiritual experience.

I believe that attention to physical sensation as part of spiritual realization is one of the most important aspects of the newly emerging spiritual understanding in the West. The use of ancient practices such as Tantric sexual techniques, drumming circles, certain types of chanting, and some of the martial arts cultivates physical sensation, as do various forms of movement therapy. We can also realize the essential quality of physical sensation by attuning to it directly within the pervasive space of fundamental consciousness or by accessing the bottom of the subtle core of the body.

Over the years that I have been teaching the Realization Process, I have found that, in general, people have more difficulty attuning to the essential quality of physical sensation than to the emotion and awareness aspects of fundamental consciousness. Although they can access physical sensation within their bodies, they are familiar with only a minimal degree of this experience. They have not felt nearly the depth of sensation that is available to them.

In order to understand what I mean by the essential quality of physical sensation, you need to be able to distinguish ordinary physical sensations from emotions. For example, you can take a moment to remember the feeling of sadness. Let yourself feel the particular tone of this experience and the aspects of yourself that are involved in the experience. Now remember feeling cold. Coldness is a physical sensation, not an emotion. Let yourself compare the tone and the particular aspects of your being involved in feeling cold to the those involved in feeling sadness. Some scientists do speak of emotions as if they were physical sensations, because they are experienced in the body. But careful attunement to these experiences reveals that they involve two different aspects or "levels" of our being.

For many people, it is necessary to release defensive holding patterns and limiting beliefs about sexuality before they can attune to the spiritual dimension of physical sensation. Traditional religions, in presenting ethics as a sexually repressive code of behavior, have been responsible for much of our difficulty in attuning to physical sensation. The taboo against sensuality has very often been augmented in people's childhoods with the threat of God's anger and rejection, or even with Hell, creating a seemingly impassable barrier between physical sensation and spirituality. Even if our families did not hold these religious ideas, the vestiges of this misguided morality still linger in our culture, a legacy of fragmentation between our upper and lower bodies that is mirrored from one generation to the next. It persists as a deeply engrained, and often unconscious, belief that physical sensation is not as important or as noble an aspect of ourselves as the qualities of love and awareness.

However, fundamental consciousness is a dimension of wholeness. To attempt to realize this dimension by attuning only to awareness and love is like attempting to divide the blue tip of a candle flame from its orange base. To live in the spiritual dimension of life is to be able to truly enjoy ourselves in the innate and inseparable arenas of wisdom, love, *and* sensual pleasure.

The Essential Qualities of the Human Form

We can experience the three essential qualities of fundamental consciousness pervading all forms in nature. In the human form, we can distinguish a more delineated spectrum. That is, the qualities of physical sensation, emotion, and awareness become, in our human anatomy, the qualities of gender, sexuality, power, love, voice, and understanding. These are the qualities that are enfolded in our being, which deepen and develop as we realize fundamental consciousness. They are also the qualities of our self-expression and our mutual contact with other human beings.

People are sometimes surprised that I include gender as a quality of fundamental consciousness. But gender is part of the qualitative experience of being fully in our bodies. Attuning to the quality of gender does not mean that we have to feel "feminine" or "masculine." It means that we can inhabit our pelvis and genital areas and feel the qualitative dimension of these parts of our body.

Gender is an important political issue, an issue of freedom to be ourselves without social persecution. Many people reject the idea of being a specific gender because they want to think of themselves as "gender fluid." But they usually mean by this that they want to have access to a full range of personality traits and behaviors that have been culturally stereotyped as male or female. All of our lives, we are shown distorted and extremely limited images of both men and women. Many of us grow up fearing that we will have to give up the many personal traits and abilities we possess that do not fit these cultural stereotypes if we identify ourselves as men or women. As children, we may fear that our lives will repeat the dilemma of our same-sex parent, for example, the depressed helplessness of our mothers or the isolation and rage of our fathers. As we become older, we notice that this dilemma extends beyond our own home. It seems to take an enormous effort of will to disassociate oneself from the vulnerable, domesticated, overly eroticized object that our society expects a woman to be or the emotionally pent-up, explosive, overly responsible worker image that is expected of a man. Hoping to win ourselves the right to be whole, free human beings, we may close off our attunement to our sexual anatomy. These defenses are meant to obliterate the feeling of being male or female. But we cannot become either whole or free by suppressing a part of our own being.

The ability to experience the quality of gender has nothing to do with limiting our personality in this way, nor does it dictate our choice of sexual partners. It means that we are inhabiting the genital and pelvic area of our body. Lack of attunement to this area will diminish our contact with both ourselves and others. The quality of gender is particularly important to include in our self-attunement because it is an aspect of being that many people constrict.

Wherever we are able to inhabit our body as fundamental consciousness, we gain the optimal functioning of that part of ourselves. In other words, as we inhabit our throat, we gain more use of our voice; as we inhabit our brain, we gain more use of our mental faculties. Just as in the broader division of awareness, emotion, and physical sensation, each of these qualities pervades our whole body.

Direct Transmission

Since no one is ever completely open to the spiritual dimension, there will be some areas of mutual contact and some areas of resistance and conflict even between two people who have realized fundamental consciousness. One of the ways in which relationships serve as a spiritual path is in helping the partners release the defenses that obstruct their realization of fundamental consciousness. An intimate relationship calls on our capacity for understanding, love, and physical sensation. As we come to know and trust another person, the protective rigidities that we have created in ourselves are gradually surrendered. We are able to receive the stimulation of another person's emotion, awareness, and sensation more and more deeply into our own being. The mutual stimulation of awareness, emotion, and physical sensation deepens both partner's realization of fundamental consciousness through a process that is known in Eastern traditions as direct transmission.

Direct transmission usually refers to the relationship between spiritual teachers and their students. Just by being in the presence of a realized teacher, our own consciousness begins to resonate with the consciousness of the teacher. The extraordinary openness of a spiritual master can help to dissolve the holding patterns that obstruct our own realization. Many people have experienced, as I have, the phenomenon of their own heart softening in the powerful love of a spiritual teacher.

Direct transmission is actually a universal principle of human relationship and occurs, to some degree, whenever two people interact. For example, if a person is more attuned to the quality of awareness than their partner is, the relationship will increase the partner's attunement to the quality of awareness. This transmission happens automatically, as a result of the contact between two people. In an ongoing relationship, the transmission will have a lasting effect.

There are many theories about what causes people to become attracted to each other. As attraction seems to be a very complex event, most of the theories are probably at least in part correct. For example, Harville Hendrix has popularized the idea that we are drawn to people who remind us of our parents, particularly in ways that caused us some emotional pain in our childhood.[4] According to this theory, the operative force of the attraction is the innate desire to resolve the conflicts and heal the wounds that have created problems and deficits in our own being. In other words, we are drawn to the person who has the potential for helping us to grow.

I believe that another, similar basis of attraction between sensitive people involves the pattern of openness to the essential qualities of fundamental consciousness. When one partner is more attuned to a quality than the other, there will be the direct transmission described above, as well as conflict and the potential for growth. Sensitive people are sometimes drawn to partners who are open in ways that they are not, through the same desire for growth and wholeness that motivates us on the psychological level. Even if this is not the basis of attraction, these differences in spiritual openness, and their resultant conflicts, can be regarded as opportunities to progress on the spiritual path.

We are also attracted to people who are open in the same qualities that we are, because the degree of mutual contact in these areas makes a relationship satisfying and pleasurable. When two people are open in the same qualities, they can touch and see into each other deeply in those aspects of being. We feel both kinship and passion with a person who can meet us in the same depth that we know ourselves.

But I do not think there is any way to explain completely why we are more attracted to some people than others. This remains part of the mystery of life. Although we can experience intimate contact with anyone in the oneness of fundamental consciousness, there will always be some people we are more drawn to than others. This natural function of attraction, wherever it comes from, becomes easier to detect if we remain open to life, if we do not bring preconceived ideas of who we want to be with into our encounters with other people. Then we can experience our true responses to other people; we can feel the actual excitement of our mind, emotions, and sexuality.

Our pattern of openness and defense is expressed continuously. It affects every aspect of our communication, including the quality of our touch, the expression in our eyes, the sound of our voice. If we listen carefully to people's speech, for example, we will hear where they are most open in their bodies. We can tell if they live mostly in their mental functioning or in their emotions or in physical sensation. The sound will also change with the content of the message, but there will be an underlying quality that does not change (except through psychological and spiritual growth) and that reflects the personality of the speaker. These expressions of openness and defense give us a subtle or even subliminal knowledge of the other people in our lives.

Exercises

These next three exercises work with the essential qualities of fundamental consciousness. Attuning to them with a partner can help you relate to each other with your whole being. We cannot realize fundamental consciousness if we leave out part of this spectrum of qualities, because this unified essence of ourselves is a dimension of wholeness. So these exercises may be the key to your mutual awakening.

EXERCISE 8 ATTUNING TO THE QUALITIES OF FUNDAMENTAL CONSCIOUSNESS

Sit facing each other, either on cushions or chairs, with your backs straight. Both people follow the instructions at the same time.

Repeat the end of exercise 1: Feel that you are inside your whole body. Find the space outside your body. Experience that the space inside and outside your body is the same, continuous space. Experience that the space pervading your body also pervades your partner's body. (Remain in your own body, as you attune to the space that pervades you both.)

Now attune to the quality of awareness. This means to become aware that you are aware. You can attune to this quality in the upper third of your body and above your head.

Experience the quality of awareness pervading your whole body. Feel that your whole body, all the way through the internal depth, is made of the quality of awareness.

Attune to your own quality of awareness and your partner's quality of awareness at the same time. The field of awareness pervades and receives you both.

Attune to the quality of emotion. You will probably notice that you automatically move your attention down to the middle third of your body as you attune to the quality of emotion.

Experience the quality of emotion pervading your whole body. Feel that your whole body, all the way through the internal depth, is made of the quality of emotion.

Attune to your own quality of emotion and your partner's quality of emotion at the same time. The field of emotion pervades and receives you both.

Attune to the quality of physical sensation. You can attune to this quality in the bottom third of your torso and legs. Bring your attention as far down in your torso and legs and as deeply into the quality of physical sensation as you can.

Experience that the quality of physical sensation pervades your whole body. Feel that your whole body, all the way through the internal depth, is made of the quality of physical sensation.

Attune to your own quality of physical sensation and your partner's quality of physical sensation at the same time. The field of physical sensation pervades and receives you both.

Now attune to the qualities of awareness and physical sensation at the same time, feeling them pervade your whole body. Bring in the quality of emotion as well, feeling it pervade your whole body. These qualities become indistinguishable from each other as you attune to all three at once. They become a fourth quality—that is, the quality of beingness, of presence. It is the qualitative aspect of fundamental consciousness. Fundamental consciousness can be experienced as emptiness or as this quality-rich field.

Attune to this mix of awareness, emotion, and physical sensation in yourself and your partner at the same time. This rich space pervades and receives you both.

Sit with your partner in this attunement for a few moments. Let your breath pass smoothly through the space of your body, without disturbing your attunement to the awareness, emotion, and physical sensation of fundamental consciousness.

EXERCISE 9 ATTUNING TO THE ESSENTIAL QUALITIES OF THE HUMAN FORM

Sit facing each other on cushions or chairs, with your backs straight. Both people follow the instructions at the same time. This exercise can also be practiced in the *yab yum* position, in which (for heterosexual couples) the woman sits on the man's lap, facing him. The yab yum position can be practiced sitting cross-legged, with the woman's legs wrapped around the man's pelvis, or sitting in a chair.

Begin by focusing on your breath, until the breath is calm and even. The inhale and exhale should be the same duration.

Feel that you are inside your feet and legs—that you inhabit your feet and legs.

Feel that you are inside your pelvis—that you inhabit your pelvis. Attune to the quality of your gender, however that feels to you. Bring your breath down into your pelvis and let it pass through the quality of your gender.

Attune to the quality of your gender and your partner's gender at the same time. Stay within your own pelvis as you do this attunement.

Feel that you inhabit your midsection, between your pelvis and ribs, including the solar plexus area beneath your ribs. Attune to the quality of your power, your personal strength, inside your midsection. Bring your breath down into your midsection and let it pass through the quality of power.

Attune to your own quality of power and your partner's quality of power at the same time. Stay within your own midsection.

Feel that you are inside your chest. Attune to the quality of love inside your chest. Bring your breath down into your chest and let it pass through the quality of love.

Attune to your own quality of love and your partner's quality of love at the same time. Stay within your own chest.

Feel that you are inside your shoulders, arms, and hands.

Feel that you are inside your neck. Attune to the quality of your own voice, your potential to speak, inside your neck. Bring your breath down through your neck and let it pass through the quality of your voice.

Attune to your quality of voice and your partner's quality of voice at the same time. Stay within your own neck.

Feel that you are inside your head and inside your whole face.

Feel that you are inside your brain, both hemispheres of your brain. Attune to the quality of your understanding inside your whole brain. Bring your breath through your brain and let it pass through the quality of understanding.

Attune to your own quality of understanding and your partner's quality of understanding at the same time. Stay within your own brain.

For advanced spiritual practitioners: Attune to the space above your head. (There is no attunement to a particular quality for this space.) Attune to the space above your own head and above your partner's head at the same time.

Feel that you are inside your whole body at once. Experience that you are one unified being inside your body. Attune to the quality of self inside your whole body. Bring your breath into your whole body and let it pass through the quality of self.

Attune to your own quality of self and your partner's quality of self at the same time.

Note: Please remember that these attunements are exercises for stretching the essential qualities. Do not hold on to these qualities when you have finished the exercise. Let yourself settle into your natural state.

EXERCISE 10 TOUCHING WITH THE ESSENTIAL QUALITIES

Sit upright with your eyes closed. One partner has their hands resting with palms up on their knees. The other partner places their hands palms down on their partner's hands, so that the palms are touching. Inhabit your pelvis. Attune to the quality of gender inside your pelvis. Touch each other's hands with the quality of gender. (You may feel that the quality you are attuning to in your body automatically affects the quality of your touch.)

Inhabit your midsection, between your ribs and your pelvis. Attune to the quality of power inside your midsection. Touch each other's hands with the quality of power.

Inhabit your chest. Attune to the quality of love inside your chest. Touch each other's hands with the quality of love.

Inhabit your neck. Attune to the quality of your voice. Touch each other's hands with the quality of your voice.

Inhabit your whole brain. Attune to the quality of your understanding. Touch each other's hands with the quality of your understanding.

Inhabit your whole body. Attune to the quality of self in your whole body. Touch each other's hands with the quality of self.

V

BARE PERCEPTION
How Unified Consciousness
Transforms the Senses

*The mountains, rivers, earth, grasses, and trees are
always emanating a subtle, precious light, day and night,
always emanating a subtle precious sound,
demonstrating and expounding to all people the unsurpassed truth.*

YUAN-SOU

IN 1981, WHILE LIVING at a Zen monastery in upstate New York,
I met a Yugoslav musician named Zoran, who is now my husband.
One of the things that attracted me to him was a quality of alert
silence that seemed to surround him like a field of radar. In one
of our first encounters, we were sitting on a bench at the edge of
the forest, just as the crickets began their evening uproar. With our
heads in close proximity, my hearing was stretched open by his
sensitivity to sound. The insects' brassy song became an exquisite
pattern of tiny discernible distances.

In the previous chapters, I have described how our capacities
for awareness, love, and physical sensation deepen and unify as
we realize spiritual oneness. As our subjective organization—our
defenses and other holding patterns—of these capacities dissolves,

so does our sense of being a subject separate from an objective external world. Our own being is experienced as continuous with the unified awareness, love, and physical sensation that pervades everywhere. This same transformation occurs in our senses. As we realize spiritual oneness, our perception becomes more subtle and unified. As our subjective manipulation of our perception dissolves, we realize that there is no true separation between subject and object. There is no boundary between ourselves as the perceiver and that which we perceive. All of our perceptions arise directly out of the unified empty space of fundamental consciousness. In the spiritual literature of the East, this clear immediacy of the perceptible world is called "direct" or "bare" perception. An early Buddhist text describes bare perception by saying, "In the seen there will be just the seen; in the heard, just the heard; in smelling, tasting, touching, just smelling, tasting, touching; in the cognized, just the cognized."[1]

In the West, this aspect of spiritual realization has often been described as a dropping away of veils. It feels as if there is finally no barrier between ourselves and whatever we are perceiving. We are fully alert to the present moment, just as it is. This stripped-clean perception reveals a very different world from the one we used to know. The apparent solidity of our environment now appears to be transparent, permeable. This means that instead of seeing and touching just the surface of the people and things around us, we can see and touch through their internal depth. We can look at a flower and see the vibrancy of the life force within it. We can touch a person and feel the qualities of that person's being within their body.

As our perception becomes more subtle, we are able to perceive the luminosity and the qualities of aliveness and sentience that pervade the whole material world. Everything that we perceive appears to be radiant and both substantial and weightless at the same time, as if it were made of consciousness. Recently, on the last morning of a week-long Realization Process retreat, one of the participants came to the session very excited. He had been casually looking out of a restaurant window at the forest as he ate breakfast. There was a telephone pole right next to a tree. He noticed, for the first time in his life, how very much more alive the tree was than the telephone pole. In the spiritual dimension, even a blade of grass looks conscious, as if it could think and speak.

Asian metaphysics says that each sense is a type of consciousness. We do not perceive the world with the sense organs alone; our consciousness perceives the world through the organs of the senses. It is really our consciousness that sees, for example; the eyes are just the instrument of seeing. We can say that the eyes are like the lens of a camera; they do not actually take the picture. As we realize spiritual oneness, we discover that our various sense consciousnesses are actually the one fundamental consciousness that pervades everywhere. The revered ninth-century Zen master Rinzai said, "O Brethren, the Mind-Reality has no definite form. It permeates and runs through the whole universe. In the eye it acts as sight; in the ear it acts as hearing; in the nose it acts as the sense of smell; in the mouth it speaks; in the hand it grasps; in the foot it walks."[2]

As fundamental consciousness, all of our senses function together. For example, just as we are able to think and feel at the same time, we are able to see and hear at the same time. Each moment occurs as a single, multifaceted vibrational pattern that registers in all of our senses at once. Just like the movement of our thoughts, feelings, and physical sensations, our perceptions register in the stillness of fundamental consciousness without altering it. In the language of Zen, they "leave no trace." For example, the sound of a gong can reverberate through the stillness and silence of our consciousness without disturbing the stillness or silence at all. This means that the reverberation will occur in its totality, without any interference on our part.

Bare perception is entirely effortless. We do not have to look in order to see or to listen in order to hear. We need only to receive our environment exactly as it is in each moment.

Direct transmission occurs in perception just as it does in the qualities of awareness, love, and physical sensation. As I described above in my encounter with my husband, the openness of another person's perception can stretch open our own. This can happen when we see or hear a work of art. If we open to the depth and harmony of the artist's perception, we may release some of the holding patterns that limit our own capacity for perception.

The senses are also pathways of resonance and mutual contact between ourselves and other life. For example, we make eye contact with other people. And when we touch another person, we experience mutual tactile contact between that person's body and our own. This form of contact becomes increasingly subtle and pleasurable as we realize spiritual oneness. Just as two people can experience the resonance and continuity of love, awareness, or physical sensation that pervades them both, they can open to oneness through their gaze or through any of the senses. In this practice, the function of direct transmission will help both partners release the holding patterns that obstruct their perception.

Perception can function as a path toward spiritual realization in the same way that love, awareness, or physical sensation can be a path. The Buddha is said to have attained his complete enlightenment when, after sitting for many days absorbed in meditation, he opened his eyes and saw the morning star.

Since fundamental consciousness pervades our whole being, to perceive with (or as) fundamental consciousness means that we perceive with our whole being. We see, hear, touch, taste, and smell with our whole body and mind. I once attended a meditation intensive with the Zen master Joshu Sasaki Roshi. In private interviews, he tested the student's degree of enlightenment by banging a short wooden stick on the ground. He wanted to see if we could open to the full impact of the sound. There are many stories in Zen Buddhism in which a master is asked to define enlightenment and answers, "Plum blossoms in the snow," or something of that sort. Enlightenment is whatever we are experiencing in the moment, experienced with our whole being.

It is important to know that our perception shifts toward this unified, direct, and effortless experience as we realize fundamental consciousness. Otherwise, we may spend many wonderful hours shut away in meditation and then return to our fragmented state of consciousness as soon as we encounter the perceptual stimulation of our everyday lives. However, some spiritual teachers place so much emphasis on bare perception that we might conclude that spiritual realization involves only the perceptual aspect of our being. I have observed many spiritual practitioners attempting to live only in the clarity of their perception while their capacity for emotion, for example, remains constricted. Although we are never entirely without constriction, to focus only on one aspect of spiritual realization will intensify the fragmentation in our being.

To focus only on the perceptual aspect of realization may intensify a very common form of fragmentation, in which the world outside of one's body is attended to while the internal space of one's body is ignored. Spiritual practitioners, often having been particularly sensitive as children, may grow up with exactly this imbalance of focus toward the external world. The vividness of the sights and sounds around them and the changes in facial expression, vocal tone, and other emotional cues of the people in their environment distract many sensitive children from inward contact with their own emotions, thoughts, and physical sensations. It is then only too easy to continue to fine-tune this perceptual vigilance through spiritual practice. We cannot actually arrive at fundamental consciousness through practicing bare perception alone, without opening all of the capacities of our being.

Unveiling the Senses

There are many ways in which we limit or veil our perception. One of the main obstacles to bare perception is the tendency to substitute ideas for experience itself. These concepts come, for the most part, out of our past experience. Human beings are fast learners. As children, we learn that life is a certain way, that men and women and all of the various objects around us are a certain way, based on the information that first impresses itself on our minds. It is very challenging for us as adults, having learned how life is, to perceive each moment of life unfolding anew.

Our familiarity with the idea of "table," for example, obscures our actual experience of this particular table in this present moment. In order to truly experience the table, we need to receive it, without any preconception, in the clear, empty space of our consciousness. When this occurs, we realize that the table is not separate from the consciousness that reveals it. It is not separate from our perception. Our own existence and the table's existence appear to arise simultaneously out of the same consciousness.

To perceive another human being in this way is particularly challenging, and important, in ongoing relationships. Over time we tend to form an idea of who the other person is and then expect them to be that way forever. We form habitual ways of relating to people based on our static mental idea of who they are. When we receive our partner or friend in the unguarded openness of bare perception, our relationship with them is constantly renewed.

When our senses are constricted, it is easy to feel withdrawn from the limited world we perceive or to project onto it our old fears and aversions. To feel truly involved with other people, we need to truly perceive them. We need to allow ourselves to hear the sound of their voices, feel the quality of their touch, observe the expressions and attitudes that change in them from moment to moment.

Mental concepts also impede our innate function of attraction. We possess a natural capacity for arousal in our intelligence, emotions, and sexuality that draws us toward particular people. Our image of the perfect man or woman can prevent us from finding a mate by obstructing our ability to respond to the actual people we encounter. These images are often based on our personal history. For example, I worked with a woman who always rejected men whose hands looked "too smooth." Until she examined her childhood, she had not associated this rather limiting preference with her grandfather, a hard-working carpenter who had been the only positive male figure in her early years.

Our images of male and female attractiveness also emerge from the communal, cultural fantasy that is passed from one generation to the next and reinforced through the media. Cultural images are difficult to shed because they are so ubiquitous; they become as unnoticeable as background noise. To rid ourselves of these generic images of men and women requires that we allow the people in our lives to register fully in our perception. When our senses are open, we often find beauty where we did not expect it.

When we project mental concepts onto the people and things around us, we live in an abstract world. Interestingly, the realization of the spiritual dimension is a progression away from abstraction and toward an experience of specific, concrete reality. Spiritual realization is a realization of this present moment, fully lived, just as it is.

Besides the projection of concepts onto reality, we limit our perception by simply not being attentive to the moment. Anyone who has attempted to sit and quiet the mind in meditation for any prolonged period is familiar with the many ways in which we divert our attention from the present. For the most part, these are habitual patterns of distraction that we have cultivated all our lives in order to cope with anxiety and boredom. We also limit our attention in order to concentrate on particular tasks—for example, the person who dims the perceptual world in order to think without distraction—and we automatically blot out unpleasant perceptual stimuli. Over time, these fragmented or narrowed patterns of focus become fixed in the tissues of the sense organs. This often produces a vicious cycle in which we increase the rigidity of our focus in order to compensate for limitation or exhaustion in our sense organs.

Holding patterns in the sense organs can become so severe that they cause deafness or blindness. For example, I worked with a man who had accepted his deafness as an inevitable symptom of his advanced age. But as he began to contact the internal space of his body, he could clearly feel the tension that he held in the deaf ear. Although he was now retired, he had worked for many years as a television cameraman, receiving instructions through an earphone in that same ear. Meir Schneider, a man who was born blind, writes a moving account of his partial recovery of vision through relaxation exercises and through deep insight into his fear of seeing.[3] There are many reasons why people are afraid to encounter the world with clear perception. Schneider discovered that he was terrified that other people would not see what he saw, that vision would isolate him from other human beings. Some people fear that they will dislike what they see if they allow themselves to see clearly, or that they will be distracted by desire for the people and objects around them.

We created most of the rigid limitations in our perception as children, to defend ourselves against the impact of specific painful perceptual stimuli. We may, for example, shut out the sound of our parents arguing by constricting our hearing or shut down our sense of smell against a persistent odor of whisky that accompanies strange alterations in our parents' behavior. We may respond to spoken or unspoken commands against perception from adults who wish to conceal themselves from the direct scrutiny of their children. We also match the ways our parents limit their own perception by mirroring their holding patterns in our own sense organs. As adults, we may guard against fully seeing the facial expressions of the people around us, because we unconsciously fear the same expressions of anger, neediness, etc., that distorted our parents' features or the same dissonance between vocal tone and facial expression that confused us as children.

How Our Pattern of Defense Shapes our Perception

In addition to these direct defenses against perception, our sense organs are also constricted by the pattern of defense in our whole body. As I explained in the last chapter, each small part of ourselves contains both the spectrum of our essential qualities (awareness, emotion, physical sensation) and the pattern of defense within our whole organism. If we are most open in our mental capacity and most defended in our physical sensation, for example, each of our senses will contain the same pattern of openness at the top—the top of the eyes, the top of the orifices of the ears, the top of the nostril orifices (toward the tip of the nose)—and constriction at the bottom.

Although this correspondence occurs in all of our senses, it is easiest to discern in our eyes. If we look carefully at other people, we will notice that we all gaze more through some parts of our eyes than others. If we have more internal contact with our head than our pelvis, for example, we will see more out of the top of our eyes than the bottom. This will produce a different expression in our eyes than in someone who is more open in their pelvis or chest. Although this placement will change somewhat in different circumstances, most of these patterns of openness and defense are either habitual attitudes or chronic rigidities in the physical tissues of our body. In this way, we maintain specific limitations in our perception of our environment, which we mistake for the nature of reality.

The pattern of openness and defense in our sense organs determines the range of qualities in the world we perceive. For example, if we see mostly through the top of our eyes, our visual perception of the world will lack texture and weight. You can try this out yourself by looking at the carpet in your room or the fabric of your clothes. Try seeing the texture of the carpet or the clothes that you are looking at. If you observe yourself carefully as you do this, you will notice that you automatically gaze through the bottom of your eyes and contact the bottom of your body in order to see the texture.

Our holding patterns also determine the range of qualities in our sense organ contact—for example, in our eye contact or our touch. If we constrict our emotional capacity, for example, there will be a corresponding lack of emotion in the expressiveness of our eyes or our touch, in our visual or tactile contact with other life. We will not be able to see or to touch "from the heart." The information that we receive through our senses will be limited in the same way.

As we realize spiritual oneness, the holding patterns in our senses gradually dissolve, and we begin to receive the whole picture. We are able to rest in the balance of internal and external experience, and the world around us becomes increasingly vivid and meaningful. There is a mysterious and satisfying harmony in the "multimedia" experience of each moment.

The process of freeing the senses can be even more challenging than letting go of other types of holding patterns, because it actually changes the world in which we live. The new range of information available to us may require that we reexamine our life choices. There may also be some temporary blurriness of perception as we release our habitual ways of focusing, but that will dissolve into greater clarity. Some people also find it difficult to adjust to the luminosity of bare perception. I worked with one woman who would emerge from meditation waving her hands in front of her as if to disperse the excess radiance in the air. It took about a year before she became accustomed to the light-filled space as the normal appearance of the world.

It can also be difficult to shift from our abstract, imagined world to the stripped-down world of actual experience. Although I was a dancer for most of my childhood and adolescence, I experienced the main locus of my being high up in my head. From there I perceived the world around me as a moving array of symbolic meaning. Then, when I was in my twenties, a back injury forced me to enter into deeper contact with my body and self. One of the first things I noticed as I began the shift toward wholeness was that the world seemed very different. It had become more solid, more soberly "just the facts" in its look and sound and feel. Although some people feel lighter as they open to the spiritual dimension, I felt heavier, and everything around me suddenly had more substance and weight as well. I was struck by the ungraspable otherness of the world, for it was no longer tied up with my own imagination. Then, as I continued on my path, the appearance of the world continued to change. The solidity of the world became transparent. There was a creek near the monastery in upstate New York where I often went to meditate. Sitting there one day, I noticed that the rocks seemed weightless. They were both substantial and "empty" at the same time. They appeared to be made of radiant space.

Recently a friend told me sadly that after many years on his spiritual path, he is still unable to see God in everyone. My understanding is that God is in the seeing itself. As our own vision becomes the subtle, bare perception of fundamental consciousness, it sees itself in all of the beings and objects we encounter.

Another woman, who works as a cranial-sacral practitioner (a subtle form of bodywork), told me recently that she'd met a photographer who travels around the world trying to take pictures of divine light. She said that she felt she understood this photographer because her own work with people requires her to touch the divine light in the body. All of our senses can become subtle enough to detect the radiance of the spiritual dimension in other people, no matter how hidden it is. In his "Song to Naropa," the Tibetan Buddhist sage Tilopa calls this "gazing with sheer awareness into sheer awareness."[4]

Seeing Through the Body

As we realize fundamental consciousness, we gain the ability to "see-feel" through the internal space of another person's body. We can perceive, within this space, the qualities that make up their being, the streaming of energy through their body, and even the movement of their feelings and thoughts. Some very sensitive people can hear the unspoken words that a person is thinking. Some can see the internal organs in people's bodies and diagnose illnesses.

Just as we do not need to see a person's facial expression in order to detect the quality of anger or sadness in their voice, we are able to perceive emotional qualities in the body. We can discern both a person's present emotional responses and the static emotional qualities that have been held in their body since childhood. Interestingly, we do not even need to be in proximity to someone to read their emotional responses. For example, in telephone conversations we can often perceive the emotional reactions of the person we are speaking with in the silence that precedes their verbal response.

Bare perception is thus an inseparable part of our oneness and intimacy with other life. Although many people are afraid at first of what their increased perception will reveal, most find that it brings them a deep sense of kinship with other living beings. When we perceive another person this intimately, we are able to recognize in them the same innate spirit and the same painful constraints that we know in ourselves. This is an unshakable foundation for compassion. It also makes our relationships less confusing, because we can see more clearly where people are open and where they are defended. In other words, we can see "where they are coming from." As well as clarifying our connection to the people in our present lives, this clear-through perception can help us resolve important relationships from the past.

A woman named Cynthia came to work with me because she had become obsessed with a man who had left her several months before. She felt compelled to keep calling him, only to be rejected again and again. I was impressed by Cynthia's attractive, lively spirit, and I sympathized with her frustration that she was directing her considerable passion toward a man who was not interested in her. But as she narrated for me her history of relationships over the past twenty years of her adult life, it became clear that she was consistently drawn to men who rejected her. As she was well read in the field of psychology, she acknowledged that this pattern might have something to do with her relationship with her father.

I placed an empty chair opposite Cynthia and asked her to picture her father sitting on the chair. The empty chair technique comes from Gestalt therapy and is very effective for releasing bound emotions in relation to important people in our lives. But I wanted Cynthia to do something more subtle than the usual Gestalt-style dialogue. I wanted her to really see her father, to see through his body to the life within.

Cynthia stared at the empty chair, seeming to shrink in her own skin. "Can you see him there?" I asked.

"Yes." Her expressive face had taken on a pathetic quality, like a beggar.

"What do you feel when you look at him?"

She sat with this question for a while, trying to articulate a feeling that she was so familiar with but had never named. "I feel locked out," she said finally.

I led Cynthia through the basic Realization Process exercise for attuning to the clear space pervading her body and the environment. I then asked her to experience that the space pervading her body also pervaded the image of her father's body, sitting on the empty chair. "This subtle, pervasive consciousness," I told her, "is the basis of perception. Just as your consciousness pervades your father's body, so does your perception."

Cynthia was surprised to find that she could see through her father's body. I asked her to describe his chest. She sat for several moments in fundamental consciousness with her father, focusing on his chest. I watched her expression register surprise, then understanding, and then sadness.

"There is a frozenness there," she said without turning away from him, "a kind of thickness."

I asked her to focus her attention within the thickness itself. And then to see-feel the emotional tone inside the thickness. I watched Cynthia tune even more subtlely and precisely into the imaginary figure on the chair. Then she began to cry.

"There is fear in there, it is almost terror," she said, "and also longing. The same longing that I feel for him. But the fear covers it."

Cynthia felt relieved by this perception. She had always assumed that her father did not like her, that he shut her out because he found her deficient in some way. She had tried to make herself more worthy of his approval, but her efforts had never won his love. Now she could see, with her own eyes, that it was his difficulty, his own fear, that kept him from expressing love for her.

Cynthia sat for a while longer with the image of her father in the chair. She practiced being with him without making herself smaller or holding her breath. She let herself feel the longing in her own chest and in her father's chest, and recognize that his inability to love her was not a personal rejection of her. This would help her begin to let go of the effort to win his love. It would also help her let go of the compulsion to replay this confusing, painful relationship with the current men in her life.

When we see people clearly, we cease to perceive them as generic types or to respond to them based on our associations with generic types of people. For example, someone who feels insecure about his own intelligence might classify anyone with an advanced education as an "intellectual" and proceed to relate to them with fear and resentment. Bare perception means that we allow each person we encounter to register in our senses in all of their complexity and uniqueness. We experience and respond to them directly, as they appear to us at that moment, without preconceptions.

We are also able to see through the distorted images that people project of themselves. We can distinguish fantasy from actuality, sentimentality from love, inflation from power, or provocative posturing from true sexuality. When we are able to see beyond these images we can no longer be manipulated by them, and we lose our fear of them.

Recently I worked with a woman who was preparing herself for a confrontation with her ex-husband concerning the care of their teenaged daughter. Suzanne described her husband as a very powerful man. She knew that she would have to fight for what she wanted, but she was afraid that he would easily overpower her.

I gave Suzanne the same exercise I gave Cynthia, placing an empty chair across from her and asking her to attune to fundamental consciousness pervading both her and an image of her ex-husband seated there. Suzanne had great difficulty picturing her ex-husband in the chair. She was afraid to look at him, even in her imagination. She could only picture him there if she herself turned sideways away from him; she was unable to face him. This made her even more agitated about her impending meeting with him.

I told Suzanne to dissolve the image of her ex-husband, and instead, I sat down in the chair facing her. I asked her to attune to fundamental consciousness pervading both herself and me. Then I instructed her to bring her focus into the midsection of her body, between her pelvis and her ribs, and to inhabit that part of her body as deeply and fully as she could. When she had done this, I asked her to attune to the quality of power in her midsection. Carefully, and with a self-deprecating incline of her head, she let herself feel the quality of power in her midsection. Next I asked her to see-feel the same quality of power inside my midsection. To her amazement, she was able to do this too.

Now I entered into a battle of power with her, increasing the intensity of the power in my body (we have a volume control on all of these qualities) and asking her to match or better me with the intensity of her own power. Suzanne proved to be quite good at this game. She straightened her head and matched me belly for belly until we were two very powerful women facing each other.

Although to an onlooker it would seem that we were both seated very peacefully and at ease, the true power in the body is very effective in our interactions with people. In fact, it is much stronger than the pretense of power that most intimidating people display. To demonstrate this to Suzanne, I now inflated my upper body into the image that most of us associate with the powerful or overpowering person. It is the image of a bully. Suzanne quickly turned away from me. "That's just what he looks like," she said, with her face still averted.

"I'm going to hold this pose," I told her, "and you see if you can face me again and tune back into your real power." Suzanne followed these directions slowly, and I waited until she was again the powerful woman that had played matching midsections with me. "Now," I said, holding myself in the inflated attitude, "make sure that you are attuned to fundamental consciousness pervading both yourself and me. And let yourself really see me, all the way through my body." As Suzanne did this, I felt her regain her sense of power and ease.

"What do you see?" I asked.

"There is no power in you," she said. "It is only muscular tension holding an attitude. There is no power in your body."

All of the genuine qualities of our being are expressed effortlessly, without our having to impress them upon other people. In fact, they only emerge when we let go of our manipulation of ourselves and others. When we experience people in the clear space of fundamental consciousness, we can easily discern the layering of images and attitudes that obscure essential being.

Sometimes people try to restrain their perception as it becomes more subtle so as not to be intrusive toward other people. As I described in Chapter 2, we can invade another person's space by projecting our focus and energy into their body. However, the bare perception of fundamental consciousness does not involve any projecting of ourselves into other people. In fact, the more we inhabit our own body, the more subtle our perception becomes. Bare perception is the natural and inevitable result of spiritual oneness. We cannot suppress our perception without limiting our own maturity. We can, of course, refrain from being intrusive in the way we relate with other people, which often means keeping one's observations to oneself. It is also good to keep in mind that we are never (or not for a very long time) without any subjective coloration, so however clear our perception seems to us, it must still be considered our own personal view.

I have found, however, that we usually feel great relief when we are clearly perceived, even if the actual content of the perception is not verbalized. When someone sees us deeply and compassionately, we can feel the warmth and the illumination of that person's gaze, all the way through our body or being. It can help us see ourselves with the same degree of insight and acceptance. Being truly seen is one of the most healing factors in the relationship between a therapist and client or between a spiritual teacher and student. It is also one of the most healing functions of intimate relationships.

Exercises

Exercise 11 is a practice of seeing and hearing with (or as) fundamental consciousness. There is really no exercise for developing this; it is just a matter of knowing that this is possible and allowing yourself to experience it. It means letting go of your fixed ways of seeing and hearing, and allowing the full impact of the sounds and sights to register in the field of consciousness. Working with the senses in this way is an important part of realizing fundamental consciousness. We have such strong habits of perception that they can hold us in a fragmented relationship with our environment.

In this exercise, you practice shifting from your ordinary dualistic perception to allowing the unified field of consciousness (pervading both the seer and the seen, the hearer and the heard) to do the seeing and hearing. As this shift occurs, all of your senses become both unified (for example, you can see and hear at the same time) and more subtle. This subtle perception is able to see-feel the internal space of all forms of life.

Exercise 12 is an exercise for seeing and feeling the internal space of another person. Sometimes people feel that it is impolite or invasive to do this. But I believe that as long as we do not project ourselves energetically into the body of the other person, we are not being intrusive. It is fine to cultivate as much sensitivity to other people as you can. The ethical issue is what you do with the information you perceive. It is important to hold this information lightly, to always keep in mind that you may be either misperceiving or misinterpreting what you perceive. It is also important to understand that what you perceive may be more confusing than beneficial for the other person, and it is often best to keep the information to yourself. Even practicing this exercise with an intimate partner, I suggest that you be cautious about what you share of your perceptions. This exercise is for the person doing the perceiving, in order to develop your sensitivity and attunement to your partner.

EXERCISE 11 BARE PERCEPTION

Sit upright with your eyes open. Begin by attuning to fundamental consciousness: feel that you are inside your whole body at once. Find the space outside your body. Experience that the space inside and outside your body is the same, continuous space; it pervades you.

Experience that the space that pervades your body also pervades the walls of the room and everything in the room. Be sure to remain within your own body as you experience this.

Let yourself hear all the sounds in your environment. Experience that the pervasive space is doing the hearing. You do not have to listen in order to hear; the sounds simply occur in the space. The sounds are changing vibrational patterns that occur in the space without altering the space in any way. In other words, the space remains motionless as the sounds move through it. Even subtle "white noise," like the electrical hum in the house, is pervaded by the stillness of space. You are hearing with your whole self, your whole body and mind.

Now experience that the pervasive space is doing the seeing. Let your own visual field dissolve and become one with fundamental consciousness. You do not have to look in order to see; all of the visual images will appear in the space without any effort on your part. Just like the sounds, they are vibrational patterns that occur in the space without changing the space in any way. It is helpful to practice this with moving objects, such as leaves moving in the wind, or a flickering candle flame. Let the movement occur without disturbing the motionless expanse of your consciousness. You are seeing with your whole body and mind.

Let yourself see and hear at the same time. Again the sounds and visual stimuli occur and move through the absolute stillness of your consciousness. Let yourself receive these patterns in your consciousness just as they are.

Now sit facing your partner. Experience that the space pervading your own body also pervades the body of your partner. Be careful to remain within your own body as you attune to the space pervading both of you.

Allow yourself to perceive your partner with the pervasive space of fundamental consciousness. Do not focus on any specific part or aspect of your partner, but let your partner register as a whole in the open space of your consciousness. Experience that fundamental consciousness pervades and reflects all of the vibrational patterns that make up the appearance, sounds, smells, emotions, thoughts, and sensations of your partner.

EXERCISE 12 SEEING THROUGH THE BODY

Sit facing your partner with your eyes open. Your partner can keep his or her eyes closed. Again, feel that you are inside your whole body all at once. Find the space outside your body. Experience that the space inside and outside your body is the same, continuous space. Now experience that the space that pervades your body also pervades the body of your partner. You are both pervaded by the same space of fundamental consciousness.

Bring your attention to the space pervading your partner's head. Be sure to stay attuned to the space pervading your whole body and the whole body of your partner as you do this. *Do not project your focus into your partner's head.*

Let yourself see-feel-hear the internal space of your partner's head. See if you can experience where your partner is more open and where more defended within their head (some people live more on the left or right side of their head; some inhabit the crown of their head more than the base of their skull, or vice versa). Now let yourself perceive the quality of your partner's intelligence (this will feel something like the quality of your own intelligence, but not exactly the same). Let yourself see-feel what it is like to be this person inside their head.

Bring your attention to the space pervading your partner's chest. Again, do not project your focus into your partner's chest. Let the pervasive space itself do the seeing. Let yourself see-feel-hear the internal space of your partner's chest. Again, you will, with practice, be able to discern where your partner is closed or open in their chest, and the quality of their love. You will also be able to feel the qualities of any emotions that may be held in their chest, such as childhood sadness or chronic anxiety. Let yourself see-feel what it is like to be this person inside their chest.

You can repeat this exercise with your partner's midsection and pelvis.

Partners can take turns being the one who does the seeing and the one who is seen. When both partners feel comfortable with this subtle perception, you can practice seeing within each other at the same time.

VI

COMPASSION
How Relationships Can
Heal Old Wounds

But one man loved the pilgrim soul in you,
And loved the sorrows of your changing face

WILLIAM BUTLER YEATS,
"WHEN YOU ARE OLD"

COMPASSION IS ONE of the primary lessons of the spiritual path. It is through the awakening of compassion that we are able to feel genuine concern for the well-being of everyone we encounter and for all of nature. Through compassion we are able to abandon our own agendas; we are able to listen and respond with an open heart and a clear mind in all of our interactions. We become conduits for the spontaneous unfolding of circumstances toward healing and growth.

Compassion is essential for intimate relationships. It allows us to love in the face of imperfection and obstruction. It allows us to love that which is different from our own personality. It allows us to love even when our own expectations and desires are not being satisfied. And it helps us to accept the needs and changes that occur as our partner continues to grow, to love and honor our partner's "pilgrim soul." Since we cannot be truly intimate with another person without the element of compassion, intimate relationships can be powerful vehicles for developing this crucial aspect of spiritual maturity.

Compassion for the Wounded Child

All relationships have problems, and they are usually the problems that we most need to face for our own growth. We are often most attracted to a partner who fits the specific rifts in our relationships with the people we loved and depended upon in our childhood. Through compassion for both ourselves and our partner we can heal this rift; we can dissolve the barriers that have limited our contact with ourselves and other people.

As a therapist working with couples, I have seen countless examples of the healing power of compassion. When Lenny and Sharon first came to work with me, they wanted me to help them separate. After six months of living together, it was clear to them that they were "incompatible," Lenny explained to me, but they could not bring themselves to actually part. They sat at opposite ends of the couch in my office, Sharon looking cool, contained, and determined, Lenny expressing outrage in the restless movements of his arms and legs. "It's just sick that I'm still with this guy," Sharon began, and Lenny, without missing a beat, came back with, "She's sick all right." Sitting across from them, though, it seemed to me that the tension in the space between them on the couch contained more sadness and longing than animosity. I suggested to them that their conflicted state might be a sign of potential growth in their relationship, rather than separation. Lenny looked somewhat hopeful at this, but Sharon disagreed immediately. "Lenny is verbally abusive toward me," she said with finality. "I won't allow him to abuse me anymore."

Over the next few weeks, Sharon described Lenny's relentless sarcasm toward her. Lenny complained that Sharon couldn't "take it," that she would simply collapse in tears rather than stand up to him. Sharon's tears infuriated him. He felt that she was manipulating him into feeling bad about himself. He responded by becoming even more abusive toward her, so that the relationship endlessly cycled, like a dog chasing its own tail.

Then one session, when this pattern had become quite clear to all of us, Sharon suddenly had a memory of her father hitting her. Sharon's father had died when she was six. Up to now, she had described him to me as warm and playful, although she had an unusual scarcity of memories about him and about her early childhood in general. Now she had an image of his face contorted in rage and the memory of his large hand slapping her face. As she described this, Sharon began to tremble with fear, and she brought her hands up protectively to her face. The gesture brought the memory into sharper focus. "He's telling me not to talk back to him," she said. "To never, ever talk back to him." Sharon began to cry softly, as if still afraid to make any noise, and Lenny quietly slid toward her on the couch and put his arm around her shoulders.

In that session, Lenny understood why Sharon responded to his anger with tears. As a result, he began to relate to her with far more care. He also understood that Sharon's tears were not a cold manipulation of him, but a genuine reaction to his behavior. In the weeks that followed, Sharon also had a chance to see the source of Lenny's anger and to become acquainted with the wounded little boy who had suffered the same abuse from his father that he now directed toward her. This made her less afraid of Lenny. She found that she could stand up to him and talk back when he was sarcastic with her, because she had seen that he was as vulnerable as she was. This not only brought Sharon and Lenny closer to each other, but it also helped them both to heal some of their deepest psychological wounds.

To experience intimacy with another human being, we need, first of all, to feel compassion for the poignant, universal drama of a child's innocent expectation of love—in a world where love is almost always caged within a labyrinth of defenses. As young children, we created our own labyrinth of defenses, attitudes, and beliefs in order to accomplish the task of finding love and recognition within the intricate mazes of our parents' hearts. We need to understand our present relationship as the interface of two labyrinths that have been carried forward from childhood. We may find that we have not only sympathy, but also admiration for the struggles of both our partner and ourselves as we persist through the winding corridors of disappointment, loss, terror, and outrage toward the possibility of intimacy.

The walls of these labyrinths are made of memory; they are phantom structures relevant only to the past. The power of these unconscious memories dissipates when they are exposed to our present-day consciousness, acceptance, and love. Just as it is important for our own growth to know our own personal history, it greatly facilitates intimate relationships for the partners to know each other's history. Psychological maturity is achieved through healing and releasing the memories of childhood wounds that are bound in our mind, energy, and body. In an intimate relationship, we need to bring the same liberating force of love and acceptance to the wounded child that is bound in the mind and body of our partner. The recognition of the influence of the past on our partner's present-day behavior, even when our partner becomes the specter of our own deepest pain, can help us view his or her behavior with compassion and can open the path to love.

Whenever we become closely involved with another person, the possibility of love brings our unfulfilled childhood needs clamoring to the surface. If we were angry toward our original source of love, if we needed to protect ourselves from rejection or abuse, if we had to suppress our own identity for the sake of love—whatever our childhood situation—we will attempt to mold our new relationship to fit the original template so that we can at last resolve the old relationship and heal our wounds. This mechanism, which is part of the inherent healing capacity of the universe, is also the undoing of many intimate relationships.

The usual response, when our partner reveals him- or herself to be just like the old nemesis of our childhood, is to react with the same defenses that we formed in the original relationships. One reason that intimate relationships can produce such intense, protracted fighting is that both partners are so practiced at the particular battle in which they again find themselves. They are each fighting the primal battle of their lives, the stakes being, as they were in childhood, the right both to be loved and to fully exist.

The shift from protective or aggressive reactive behavior to compassion for each other's wounds is a spiritual lesson. It requires us to observe the relationship clearly without becoming lost in the siren's call of our childhood pain. Once we have attuned to the dimension of fundamental consciousness, it becomes much easier to achieve this clarity of perception and to apply the healing properties of compassion to the problems in our relationship.

So far I have emphasized the importance of having compassion for the psychological wounds of one's partner. But for many people, it is more difficult to accept compassion than to feel it for someone else. To receive compassion means revealing the fragile, unresolved aspects of ourselves that we usually keep hidden from other people and sometimes from ourselves as well. Often in a relationship, the give and take of compassion is imbalanced. One partner holds the position of the understanding caretaker, while the other partner maintains the role of needy child. Over time, this imbalance usually results in mutual resentment.

One couple, for example, came to work with me because after several months of living together, they had found themselves feeling increasingly hostile toward each other. Melissa was a successful novelist with a forceful, direct expressiveness. Sam was a talented painter, but bouts of depression had limited his creative output and the thought of trying to sell his work terrified him. He had an appealing gentleness but seemed preoccupied, as if focused on some indefinable quandary. Melissa's attitude was "Maybe you can help him. I give up." Sam's attitude was that of the noble political prisoner, determined to endure the hour without giving up his secret.

So it was Melissa who told me their story. She said that they had spent a year getting to know each other before moving in together. She had never felt so close to a man before, and he had seemed to feel the same toward her. But as soon as Sam had moved into her house, he had begun to brood. She said his depression was like a "cocoon of dark fog that absorbed him completely." He complained of her "overwhelmingly powerful" personality, but he depended on her to handle all the details of his life. She paid the bills, made the meals, kept the car running, did the banking, even made dental appointments for him. "But the worst," Melissa said, beginning to cry, "is that he won't let me help him feel better. He won't let me comfort him." At this, Sam seemed to pull even further inward, and it was, as Melissa had described, like fog thickening. "But you know what?" she said, directing her words toward Sam as if they could pierce through to him, "I don't buy it. You think you're weaker than I am, but only a very powerful man could create such an impenetrable fortress around himself."

I agreed with her. Their strength seemed evenly matched, but they needed a way to balance their expression of it. I decided to give them an exercise to do at home that would help them both experience the roles of caretaker and child. The exercise is from a form of psychotherapy called "reparenting," in which the therapist acts as a stable, loving parent while the client is allowed to regress to early childhood or infancy. This variation for couples works best if there is already a fairly close bond between the partners.

Every day, for several weeks, Melissa and Sam took turns holding and rocking each other. The person being rocked was allowed to become very young and helpless in the other's arms. Sam said that he found it very comforting to surrender to Melissa's maternal embrace. It was also a great relief for him to be allowed to feel deep emotions with another person without being pressured to verbalize those feelings. Once, during the third week of the exercise, he found himself crying "just like a baby," trusting the safety of Melissa's love. Melissa said that Sam's trust gave her a sense of extreme tenderness and closeness with him.

It was more difficult for Melissa to be held and rocked by Sam and for Sam to assume the parental role. In the therapy sessions, Melissa worked with her memories of her parents' "spaciness," which had caused her to take on the role of caretaker in the family. She remembered waiting for her parents to pick her up after school long after the other parents had come for their children and, in general, feeling abandoned to her own resources. Gradually, she was able to relax her guardedness against this negligence and to let Sam support and nurture her. Sam was very moved to see Melissa so vulnerable. It evoked a new sense of strength and responsibility in him that carried over into his daily life.

The exercise also helped Sam and Melissa communicate more honestly with each other, because they had learned to trust each other's care. When they began to know other details of each other's childhood pain, they felt that they actually knew those children, for they had held and rocked them. They were also able to recognize the wounded child in each other's present behavior. This helped them become more tolerant of each other's difficulties in the relationship.

Intimacy with another person both evokes and alarms the carefully defended, wounded child that has been kept under wraps for so many years. One of the chief requirements of intimate relationships is that we meet this frightened, angry, grieving child with compassion and respect.

Compassion for Gender Differences

One of the biggest obstacles to intimate relationships between men and women is the difference that exists between male and female thought processes and behavior. Many writers have described these differences in books such as *He Said, She Said,* by Deborah Tannen, and *Men Are from Mars, Women Are from Venus,* by John Gray. But no matter how much we read on the subject, it is still astounding to be in relationship with someone we really care about and come up against a difference in relational style that seems to require the skill of a code-breaker, or to find that our partner has beliefs, values, goals, and needs that are very different from our own.

We cannot know for certain to what extent the differences between men and women are innate or culturally conditioned. Surely, many of the differences that were once assumed to be innate now seem to be completely bogus, such as the intellectual and moral (as Freud suggested) inferiority of women or the inability of men to nurture their children. It is not difficult to see that millennia of accumulated ignorance and exploitation have resulted in distorted and limited roles for both men and women.

One of the best books I have found on this subject is *I Don't Want to Talk About It,* by Terrence Real. He writes, "Just as girls are pressured to yield that half of their human potential consonant with assertive action, just as they have been systematically discouraged from developing and celebrating the self-concepts and skills that belong to the public world, so are boys pressured to yield attributes of dependency, expressiveness, affiliation—all the self-concepts and skills that belong to the relational, emotive world. These wholesale excisions are equally damaging to the healthy development of both girls and boys. The price for traditional socialization of girls is oppression—as Lyn Brown and Carol Gilligan put it, "the tyranny of the kind and nice." The price of traditional socialization of boys is disconnection—from themselves, from their mothers, from those around them."[1]

In our society, men are denied their ability to be vulnerable and open to other human beings. Women, by the very pressure that is put on them to be "nice" and connected with other people, are denied their connection with themselves—they abandon their own needs in order to fulfill the needs of others. Neither the men nor the women in this scenario are capable of intimacy.

The stereotypical division of skills, which robs both men and women of whole facets of their being, also contributes to difficulties in intimacy. When only men are allowed to be competent in their professions, prosperous, and assertive, and only women are allowed to be nurturing, intuitive, and artistic, the intimacy between them is inevitably hindered by mutual resentment, envy, and mistrust. Although we may be attracted to our "missing half," the natural drive in every human being to be whole will often sabotage a relationship that relies on the sacrifice of our basic potential. I believe that this terrible sacrifice of personal attributes is largely responsible for the so-called battle of the sexes, in which men and women confront their lost abilities with anger, grief, and confusion.

Compassion is the solution to the dilemma of gender differences. Just as our lovers carry the wounds of their childhood family, they also carry the frustrations, blindnesses, expectations, fears, and rigid attitudes that result from being a man or a woman in our culture.

To feel compassion for these wounds of gender requires that we shift our perspective to encompass our partner's point of view along with our own. In the previous chapter, I described the shift in perception from our fragmented self/object stance to perceiving with the all-pervasive space of fundamental consciousness. This spiritual transformation of perception is reflected in our understanding of life as well. Instead of knowing just our own point of view, we begin to see each situation in our lives as a whole, from the vantage point of every person involved.

For about a year I have been working with a man named Jack. Jack is in his midforties and has never had a lasting relationship with a woman. Although he has been very successful in his professional life and is proud that he has acquired the house, car, and bank account that he set out to achieve, he feels that his life is incomplete without a wife. But whenever Jack begins a relationship with a woman, he quickly becomes enraged with her for one reason or another and can no longer tolerate her presence in his life. Since we began our work together, I have seen him pass through several of these brief, angry affairs.

One day, hearing him describe the demise of a relationship with yet another infuriating woman, I was struck by the defiant tone of his anger. It was as if he were pitted against a powerful adversary, and, in escaping from the relationship, he had scored a hard-won, if bitter, triumph.

"Was she a very powerful woman?" I asked.

He answered me with a knowing sneer. "All women are powerful," he said, as if this were something I already knew.

"All women?" I asked.

"Yes," he said, furiously. "All women. Women have all the power."

I must have looked incredulous, because he became even more enraged. "In relationships," he said, as if speaking to a moron. "Women have all the power in sexual relationships. Women get to decide if it's going to happen or not."

As he said this, I watched him shape-shift from the powerful businessman he was in his current life to the intimidated teenage boy that he once was. Jack had already spent many sessions describing the terrors of his adolescence. He had been a sensitive, intelligent boy—in teenage parlance, a nerd. He described to me how the boys in his school had attacked him physically and verbally, ridiculing his looks, his name, his clothes, and his claim to heterosexuality. He had not said much about the girls. But now he remembered the utter torment of his early attractions, his clumsy advances and the intense shame and hurt of rejection. He also remembered that he had given up his attempt to approach girls. He recalled the exact period in his life, in his senior year of high school, when he had retreated into the aloof, scowling, chain-smoking character that had shielded him all these years. As he spoke, his fury weakened and was replaced by an expression of bewilderment and regret.

We spoke for a while about the rules that we are taught early in life concerning the way men and women, or boys and girls, are supposed to approach each other—about the pressure on boys to initiate contact, the terrible risk involved in making that first phone call and then having to provide the girl with a good time, and having to risk rejection again by initiating the first gesture of physical intimacy. And then, as the boy gets older, there is the pressure on him to please a woman sexually, the threat of humiliation if he does not prove himself to be a competent lover. Jack had taken his early fears and failures with women as signs of his personal ineptness. But as we spoke, he began to feel compassion for himself as an adolescent boy, and for men in general, constrained by traditional expectations of manhood that turn the pursuit of love into a daunting obstacle course.

Jack had always resented the power that women have in their traditional role of accepting or declining the man's request for intimacy. I asked Jack if he would like to get some sense of how these cultural roles affect girls and women. When he agreed to this, I asked him to imagine himself as an adolescent girl. Jack struggled with this idea for a moment, but finally he pulled his bulky body into the attitude of a haughty, sensual, teasing girl. Then I asked him to picture an adolescent boy across the room. "You are very attracted to this boy," I said. "What are you going to do about it?" Jack intensified his sensual pose, crossing his legs seductively and giving a pretty good imitation of the come-hither expression that most girls learn at an early age. "Well," I said, "he has glanced at you and turned away. Now what are you going to do?"

Jack suddenly looked helpless and slightly ludicrous in his seductive pose, as women often feel when their efforts are ignored. "Can I call to him?" he asked.

"You can," I answered, "but that is very forward behavior for a girl. If he rejects you, there will be the added humiliation of having crossed a line, of having transgressed the bounds of feminine decorum, when he was not even interested in you."

"So I have to wait for him to notice me," said Jack, uncrossing his legs and returning, with relief, it seemed to me, to his own gender.

"Yes," I said. "The traditional courting ritual is an equal-opportunity ordeal."

Although these traditions are gradually weakening, it will be a while before we are entirely free of their destructive influence. It is therefore important that men and women support each other as we attempt to challenge our mutual history of cultural stereotypes. This means, in particular, that women need to understand the societal pressures on men to be stoic or "cool," overly responsible, and geared for battle. We need to be patient with the incongruities and frustrations that occur as they attempt to become more emotionally vulnerable and responsive. And men need to regard the emergence of female ambition, skill, and accomplishment without the reflexive reactions of fear and competitiveness. They need to be patient with the complexities of fragility and strength, need and independence, that women often display as they attempt to become more competent and assertive.

There is a popular notion in our culture, based largely on the writings of Carl Jung, that men have a female aspect and women a male aspect of personality that needs to be integrated for psychological maturity. These male and female aspects are usually described as personality traits associated with the two genders. I believe this idea has created some confusion. For example, women naturally emanate power from the subtle core of their body, just as men do. This quality has been suppressed in women, but it still exists as part of their essence. They do not have to get in touch with their "male side" in order to experience power—they just need to access the core of their own being. And men find that when they soften the defenses in their chest, for example, they are just as emotionally responsive as women. To speak of male and female parts of the personality lends support to the limitations imposed on us by conventional images of gender behavior.

When we inhabit our whole body, we discover that both power and emotion are essential capacities of our being, regardless of gender. Our anatomy allows us to feel power in our belly and love in our heart at the same time. Thus, freedom from the stereotypes of gender helps us to develop the self-contact that is the basis of our contact with one another.

Compassion requires the ability to recognize and appreciate the conflict of authenticity and defense within each person we encounter. This poignant counterpoint of reality and defense is the condition of human life. Although we can grow toward reality, we are never entirely free of this basic human drama. In order to open to the innate movement of compassion, we need to acknowledge and accept this shared condition of humanity.

People who are sensitive to the spiritual aspect of life are usually particularly sensitive and responsive to the world around them. Their ability to see and feel the pain in other people naturally evokes their compassion. However, sensitive people may also suppress their compassion in order to protect themselves from other people's suffering. They may fear that they will be overwhelmed by other people's pain or that they will have to be responsible for alleviating it. Or they may fear that the suffering in the world is somehow contagious, that it might diminish the purity and light that they have gained through spiritual practices. Many people have told me that they "take on" the pain around them, and that this has led to illness.

These fears can prevent people from realizing and living in the dimension of spiritual oneness. However, it is the realization of fundamental consciousness that enables us to be completely open and responsive to life without mimicking the holding patterns and illnesses of other people. We can allow all of the content of life, including the vibrations of emotional and physical pain, to pass through the clear space of fundamental consciousness without altering it. This means that we can see, feel, and respond to other people's pain without being injured by it.

When people realize fundamental consciousness, they find that they can finally enjoy the full impact of their sensitivity and compassion for other people. One of the most moving examples of this transition that I have witnessed was a woman named Beth, who came to work with me several years ago. Beth was a tall, thin woman who lived and related to the world from the very top of her superior height. She was extremely courteous toward me, but chillingly distant. Her whole body was pulled in from its periphery, as if to avoid contact with the air around her. Her forehead, however, was brightly lit. From this bright summit, she literally looked down her nose at me.

In the first few months of our work together, we did not get further than the first Realization Process exercise of inhabiting the body. Beth had become accustomed to numbness, and she entered the internal space of her body with extreme caution. She often spent the whole session dwelling in one part of her body, barely breathing, trying to tolerate each new sensation of aliveness. When she was able to inhabit her whole body without feeling overwhelmed, we progressed to the exercise of attuning to the qualities of fundamental consciousness—awareness, emotion, and physical sensation. But this exercise was even more difficult for her than the first one. Although she could access the quality of awareness very easily, the instructions to attune to emotion and sensation filled her with terror. She insisted that she would rather discontinue our work than open to these two qualities.

"It just feels like too much," she pleaded with me.

"Too much what?" I asked.

"Too much pain."

"Your pain?"

This question surprised her. Whose pain could it be but her own? I suggested that she attune to the pervasive space of fundamental consciousness, inside and outside her body, and then sit with this question: was it her own pain that seemed to be too much for her?

Beth sat for several minutes, attuned to fundamental consciousness. Then she suddenly pulled herself in, away from the environment, in an extreme version of the holding pattern that she had begun to release over the past few months. "It's my mother's pain," she said with effort. "It's too much for me. I don't want to feel it." She glanced quickly at the door of my office as if gauging how quickly she could get away, but she remained seated on the couch.

She described to me how her mother had depended on her for emotional support after her father had died, how she had treated Beth as the strong one in the family, someone always available to listen to her troubles. "But they were too much for me," she said, looking away from me guiltily. "I tried at first, but I couldn't help her. As soon as I was old enough, I left home and moved as far away from her as I could." I pointed out that long before she had been able to escape geographically, she had protected herself from her mother's pain by closing off her emotional responses to the environment.

Beth agreed to revisit her childhood environment in her memory. She attuned again to the pervasive space of fundamental consciousness and imagined that this space pervaded both herself and the memory of her mother. "She's a whirlwind of angry, hungry energy," Beth said, beginning to contract again. I suggested that she keep her breath slow and even and that she simply observe her mother in the space that pervaded them both. Slowly, Beth relaxed and, concentrating on her breath, was able to sit with the image of her mother. "She wants me to soothe her," Beth said, "but I don't have to. I'm just letting her be there. I'm just letting the whirlwind spin in the space."

Now I asked Beth to attune to the quality of emotion pervading both herself and her mother. I watched her search for the emotional quality in her chest and then in her whole body. Very carefully, she attuned to the same quality in the space outside of her body, so that the image of her mother was also pervaded by it. After a moment, she began to nod her head, as if she were understanding something for the first time. "I love her," she said. "I can't solve her problems but I do love her." Beth began to cry softly, rocking back and forth as if soothing an infant. An expression of extreme tenderness and compassion came over her face, and her body softened. "I feel sorry for her, and also for myself," she said. "I love us both." The memory of Beth rocking her tall, gaunt body gently on the couch has stayed with me as one of the most beautiful images of compassion that I have ever seen.

Exercise

In this exercise, which is done with a partner, you will take turns listening to each other while attuned to fundamental consciousness pervading you both. The practice of listening without responding gives each partner a chance to express themselves without the interruption of argument and denials. For the partner speaking, it is most effective to talk about your own experience in the relationship, rather than blaming the other person or defending yourself against their accusations. Since you will not be interrupted, you can take the time to feel into whatever is disturbing you in the relationship and describe it clearly to your partner.

For the partner listening, the discipline of not responding can help you to really hear your partner. As fundamental consciousness, you may be able to experience all of the different aspects of your partner's expression—their tone of voice, the feel of their emotions within their body, when they close up defensively and when they feel more open—as well as the movement of your own responses within your body, without limiting your perception of them. This will help you both to find the truth of the difficulty in your relationship and to open yourselves to the most effective resolution.

EXERCISE 13 LISTENING IN
FUNDAMENTAL CONSCIOUSNESS

Partners sit facing each other, either on chairs or cross-legged on cushions, with eyes open.

Begin with the exercise for attuning to fundamental consciousness: Experience that you are inside your whole body all at once. Find the space outside your body, the space in the room. Experience that the space inside and outside of your body is the same, continuous space. Now experience that the space that pervades your body also pervades your partner. Be sure to stay in your own body as you experience this. Keep your breath smooth and even as you sit together in the unified space of fundamental consciousness.

Take turns speaking while the other listens. You can time your periods of speaking, so that you each take ten or fifteen minutes.

The partner who is listening remains silent and stable in the open space of fundamental consciousness, keeping their breath smooth and even. Experience that the space itself is seeing and hearing your partner.

The speaking partner says whatever occurs to them. If there is something you would like your partner to know or understand about you, you can take this time to express it.

VII

SEXUAL INTIMACY
The Spiritual Essence
of Sexuality

The ultimate is, in a very real sense,
hidden within the manifest:
the infinite is present within the finite.
PAUL EDUARDO MULLER-ORTEGA

Sex and Contact

As we realize spiritual oneness, we experience that our own body, and everything around us, is made of unified, fundamental consciousness. This realization is based on a shift in the subtlety and depth of our internal contact. As consciousness, we are able to experience ourselves all the way through the internal depth of our whole body. In this dimension, as a result of this depth of internal contact, our entire organism is capable of sexual arousal and release.

By attuning to fundamental consciousness during sex, partners can experience contact with themselves and each other at the same time, throughout the whole internal space of their bodies. As I have explained earlier, the mutual contact that two people experience in fundamental consciousness is not just a connection of one body with the other. It is an experience of resonance, of subtle communication, involving awareness, emotion, and physical sensation—all at the same time. Mutual contact during sex helps deepen both partners' realization of fundamental consciousness, as well as their intimacy with each other and the intensity of their pleasure. This is true for both heterosexual and same-sex couples.[1]

Just as in other aspects of life, fundamental consciousness does not replace physical matter and energy in the sexual encounter; it includes and pervades them. Sex is still a physical act, of course, involving caressing and the stimulating of erogenous zones. But the caresses become a much more effective means of arousal when they touch through to the actual being of the body, rather than just the physical surface.

Since fundamental consciousness is the most subtle level of ourselves, it is rarely mentioned in the psychological or even the spiritual literature on sexuality. Although most people agree that they enjoy sex more when there is tenderness or love between partners, the sex act itself is generally viewed as only physical. Sexual pleasure is regarded as the result of physical friction between the partners' sexual organs, without mention of actual contact between the sexual organs. By "contact," I mean the meeting of one being with another through the layers of energy and physical matter. Even traditional spiritual sex practices often emphasize the physical level, focusing on strange postures that can be assumed or the number and phrasing of "strokes" of the penis within the vagina to which men are advised to aspire. This is based on the understanding that the chief requirement for sexual "success" is that the man maintain his erection for long periods of time. Naturally, many men accomplish this task by diverting their attention elsewhere during sex. But when the man is distracted, both the pleasure and the spiritual potential of the sexual encounter are reduced.

The Indian, Tibetan, and Chinese spiritual traditions also contain more subtle sexual exercises that emphasize the energy dimension. These teach the exchange of energy between partners during sex, as well as ways to send the energy of sexual arousal up through the subtle core of the body toward the brain. When sexual sensation reaches the brain, it produces an experience of ecstatic release. Although these exercises work with energy, they can deepen and expand our realization of fundamental consciousness because they help open the subtle core of the body, our entranceway into spiritual oneness. The Tibetan Buddhist teacher Lama Thubten Yeshe wrote, "Practice with a consort causes the airs to enter the central channel more strongly; and the more strongly the airs enter, the more strongly they will stabilize and absorb, and the more bliss will be generated. The purpose of practicing with a consort is to increase these experiences, and eventually to energize complete absorption of the winds at the heart chakra, total bliss, and total realization of nonduality."[2]

The importance of the energy dimension for sexual intimacy has also been recognized by many schools of psychotherapy. In the 1950s, Wilhelm Reich developed a method of psychotherapy that emphasized sexual energy. Reich believed that psychological health was measured by how fully someone could experience orgasm. A truly healthy person would experience the release and pleasure of orgasm throughout his or her whole body. Reich's method, called orgone therapy, focused on freeing the energy system by releasing the psychological defenses that bind and diminish it.

Just as in other aspects of relationship, however, if partners remain in the energy dimension, they do not reach the deepest level of either intimacy or spiritual realization. The energy dimension, although of great importance to sexual intimacy, is just a partial aspect of sexual experience. Even during sexual union, the oneness that we experience in fundamental consciousness is very different from the merging that occurs in the energy dimension. Instead of the "zoned out" feeling of merging, there is an experience of presence and clarity throughout the bodies of both partners.

Also, as fundamental consciousness, we can remain present as the spontaneous flow of arousal moves through our own body and the body of our partner as it builds toward orgasm. This helps increase our threshold for sexual sensation, for if we swoon into semiconsciousness at the first whiff of pleasure, we limit our potential for arousal and release. In this dimension, we are able to remain present even during the release of orgasm. This does not mean that we watch the experience of release as if we were somehow separate from it, but that our consciousness pervades the movement and ecstasy of release. This enables us to experience the full impact of sexual pleasure. It also enables us to integrate the movement of energetic release with the stillness of fundamental consciousness. This helps us integrate fundamental consciousness with the movement of all of our life experience.

Many sexual difficulties can be resolved when we experience internal contact with ourselves and our partner in fundamental consciousness. For example, both men and women can experience a greater intensity of sexual pleasure if they inhabit and contact each other through the internal space of their genitals. Mutual genital contact also helps couples match each other's intensity of pleasure, so that the duration of the sexual encounter is satisfying for both partners.

Many sensitive people guard against sexual arousal because they are afraid of being overwhelmed by sensation. A couple once came to work with me because, in the five years that they had been together, they had never been able to enjoy having sex together. It was the wife, Paula, who had persuaded her husband,

Anthony, to come to therapy. She complained that Anthony never initiated sex with her, and when she initiated it, he almost always rebuffed her. He did not even like her to touch him affectionately. Anthony agreed that he did not like to be touched "all of a sudden" and wanted her to "warn" him before she approached.

When they did have sex, Anthony reached orgasm almost immediately, and this too felt like a rejection to Paula, as if he wanted to get it over with as quickly as possible. Paula said that Anthony's rejection of her made her feel unattractive, and she constantly demanded that he admit to his attraction to other women. But Anthony insisted that he did find Paula attractive; it was just difficult for him to be close to someone physically. Paula had also persuaded Anthony to see several hypnotists and psychics to find out if he had ever been sexually abused. But there did not seem to be any history of sexual violation in Anthony's past.

Paula was a sprightly, quick-witted woman in her thirties, capable of humorous repartee even while she was crying. Anthony, about ten years older, had a remarkably gentle, lyrical voice and a penetrating gaze that was usually directed toward the floor during our sessions, or toward the window behind me. As they spoke about their relationship, Paula sprawled on the couch, an arm or a leg extended toward Anthony, while Anthony sat almost primly upright, his hands placed carefully on his knees. It seemed to me that there was something deliberate about Anthony's self-containment, as if it were a practiced skill. I noticed that he tightened his posture, ever so slightly, every time Paula shifted her position on the couch. I had the sense that he was extremely aware of her physicality.

In one session, about a month after we had first met, I asked them to sit across the room from each other, as far as they could get from each other in my office. Then I asked Paula to stroke Anthony's body from where she sat. Although she was a little puzzled by this instruction, she faced Anthony and began to caress the air. To her surprise, she was able to feel that she was actually touching him. And Anthony was also able to feel her touch. For the first time, I saw Anthony relax his guard and receive the sensation of Paula's caress. When they reversed roles, Anthony could easily touch Paula from across the room, and Paula found that if she attuned very subtly to the space between them, she could also feel Anthony's touch. They enjoyed this exercise very much, and Paula joked that they had finally found a way to have sex. But when they did attempt to have sex that night, Anthony again recoiled from Paula's touch.

In the following sessions, I taught them how to inhabit their bodies and to experience oneness with each other in fundamental consciousness at the same time. We also continued the exercise of them caressing each other across space. As they became adept at inhabiting their own bodies, Anthony was able to receive the stimulation of Paula's touch at closer range. Finally he was able to allow her to put her hand on his body itself. They practiced touching each other and receiving each other's touch, beginning with less sexually responsive parts of the body, such as the arm or lower leg. One would rest their hand on the other's body, while the other person practiced inhabiting that area and opening to the sensation of the touch.

During this process, Anthony remembered the possessive, all-encompassing nature of his mother's embrace. He was able to observe how he "closed up" his skin when he thought of her touch. Although no one would equate the embraces of a loving mother with sexual abuse, his mother's affection had overstimulated Anthony, a very sensitive child, and overwhelmed his budding connection to himself.

After several months had passed, I gave Paula and Anthony a new exercise to practice at home. I asked them to lie next to each other, side by side, and practice inhabiting their whole body and receiving each other's touch throughout their whole body. They then progressed to practicing the same exercise facing each other. I emphasized that they should wait for sexual arousal to occur spontaneously and not to have sex unless that happened. This constraint was difficult for Paula but it helped relieve Anthony's anxiety about having to perform sexually. Finally, they both were able to relax and receive the stimulation of each other's touch, and sexual arousal did occur. They also found that Anthony was able to sustain his arousal longer when he inhabited his genital area. This allowed him to tolerate and to build a much greater intensity of pleasure than he had ever experienced before. One morning I received an email from Anthony. "This must be what all the fuss is about," it said.

The exploration of sexual healing and freedom was, I believe, one of the most important enterprises of the twentieth century. Since my adolescence in the 1960s, I have been familiar with the various rigors of this quest; I know what courage and personal strength is needed to challenge one's own inhibitions and rebel against antiquated moral codes. I have also seen the self-destructive edge of this pursuit, the overuse of sensation-enhancing drugs, the despair over one's sexual deficiencies, and the bitterness of a hunger stimulated but never quite satisfied. I think that the missing element in much of this sexual exploration has been the knowledge of our spiritual essence as the basis of contact and sexual pleasure.

Several years ago, a man came to work with me who had devoted the past three decades of his life to the pursuit of "great sex." In his fifties, Phil had long, wildly curling gray hair, and he always wore sensual fabrics like silk in bright colors, and silver jewelry. I recognized him at once, as one old hippie to another. But beneath the colorful bandana wrapped around his head, his eyes held an unchanging grimness that reflected his long, disappointing odyssey.

Phil felt that if he could experience a truly satisfying sexual encounter, it would empower him in every aspect of his life. To this end, he had attended countless workshops, learned an array of sexual techniques, and engaged in many different types of sexual orgy. With the help of drugs and alcohol, his sexual adventures had become increasingly wild. But even though he was finally able to feel fairly at ease writhing naked among a group of people, he did not experience much actual pleasure in these encounters. Furthermore, when he attempted to have sex one-on-one with someone, his old inhibitions seemed to come right back.

Although Phil was willing to practice the Realization Process exercises and was able to experience the pervasive space of fundamental consciousness fairly quickly, he dismissed my suggestions about the nature of intimacy. After several months, he announced that he was going to Thailand, something he "should have done years ago," to find the prostitute that would finally liberate him from his sexual conundrum. He returned two weeks later, a puzzled and somewhat tender expression in his eyes, and a little more interested in learning about contact. He told me that when he arrived at the establishment in Thailand, they showed him a lineup of women from which to choose. Without hesitation, Phil pointed to the youngest one, a delicate beauty, new to the job. He had always resented the legal and moral restraints in America that kept him from the having sex with someone so young. He was sure that this very young woman would have sufficient vitality to satisfy him. But when they were alone, he suddenly noticed the terror in her eyes. Although she allowed him to enter her, he could feel the fear in her body. He said that he had never been so aware of the other person in bed with him. Although she was not able to give him the sexual ecstasy that he craved, she did help him begin to heal his sexuality. Her fear and vulnerability compelled him to abandon his anxieties about himself and his demand to be satisfied, and to attune to the presence of another human being.

Sexuality and Wholeness

The development of our sexuality is necessary for spiritual realization because it is part of the wholeness of our organism. I do not mean that we must be sexually active in order to realize fundamental consciousness. But we do need to release the defenses that repress our sexuality in order to reach the subtle core of our whole body. This can be accomplished through recognizing and releasing holding patterns in the body, as described in a previous chapter. It can also be done through cultivating sexual release throughout the whole body, either through self-pleasure or with an intimate partner.

We cannot realize the wholeness and unity of fundamental consciousness if we do not include our sexuality and our essential quality of physical sensation in our subtle attunement to ourselves. As I have said, for many people the physical sensation aspect of fundamental consciousness is the most difficult to access. Sexual repression is passed down from one generation to the next through education and example. This legacy has left us, as a culture, relatively numb to the pleasure of touch and sexual arousal.

Since the latter half of the twentieth century, however, we have begun to heal and regain this lost part of ourselves. The fortunate encounter of Western psychological understanding with Asian spiritual teachings has taught us the value of nature and the basic unity and interdependence of the various parts of nature. In our time, even the rigidly conservative medical profession has begun to accept the relationship between our physical functions, emotions, and thoughts. Sexuality, once thought to be the base hunger of the body alone, is seen in this new light as belonging to and affecting our whole nature.

This must necessarily transform our spiritual understanding as well. If there is no true separation between our physical nature and our spiritual nature, then our sexuality is part of our spiritual nature. To attempt to transcend our sexuality produces a fragmentation in us, a schism that is experienced as tension and incompleteness, often leading to illness and depression. The experience of wholeness that occurs when we accept our sexuality as belonging to our essential, spiritual nature is one of the hallmarks of the new spiritual understanding that is presently emerging.

Both Western psychology and Asian religion have helped generate the perception of spiritual realization as a process of becoming whole. The Eastern religions contribute to this understanding because they teach that our true nature is spiritual. Asian spiritual methods seek to uncover our reality from the distortions that mask it, just as modern Western psychology seeks to uncover our true humanity from the repression that binds it.

Western psychology has been engaged, since it began with Sigmund Freud, with the subject of sexuality. Freud was fascinated by the coexistence of what he called the id—by which he meant all that was natural and instinctive in us—with the transcendent artifice of civilization. Freud felt that people became psychologically ill when the id threatened to break out of its civilizing containment. He saw his job as helping people sublimate these unruly natural instincts. Only gradually has the emphasis in the field of psychology shifted from the bolstering of all that is civilized in us to the salvage of all that is natural. Wilhelm Reich, with his intuition of the completely orgasmic person, was one of the first Western psychologists to recognize the importance of sexual health for personal maturity.

The relatively inclusive attitude of Asian religion toward sexuality has also helped loosen our culture's association of sexual "purity" and spiritual life. The Trappist monk Thomas Merton tells a funny story in his *Asian Journal:* One of the people he visited in India, in 1968, was the director of the International Academy of Indian Culture. At the end of his visit, he was given the choice of several cloths printed with mandalas, a geometric design that is used for meditation. Merton chose one that he said attracted him as being "very lively." When he brought it back to his hotel and examined it more closely, he found that it was covered with tiny images of men and women having sexual intercourse. He writes, "On close inspection I find it to be full of copulation, which is all right but I don't quite know how one meditates on it. It might be a paradoxical way to greater purity."[3] This design of "copulation" is known in Buddhism as "deities in union." The woman faces the man with her legs wound around his hips and her head thrown back as if in extreme sexual excitement. It is one of most sacred images of Tibetan Buddhism and is used in it's advanced visualization practices.

Several years ago, I attended a ceremony at a Tibetan Buddhist monastery near my home in Woodstock, New York. The monastery belongs to the Kagyu lineage of Buddhism, which has been compared to the Catholic Church in its use of elaborate ritual and ornate decor. The ceremony was called an "empowerment" because it authorizes and prepares the participants to do a particular practice, this one dedicated to the Medicine Buddha. The practice involves a combination of devotional prayers and transformative techniques.

The officiating lama was Khenpo Karthar Rinpoche, the abbot of the monastery, an old man of great dignity. He sat at the front of the shrine room on an elevated chair decorated with rich brocades, while the sixty or so participants sat cross-legged on cushions facing him. In the main event of the ceremony, the lama gave us the blessing of the Medicine Buddha for our "body, speech, and mind." For this, he came down from his throne and walked slowly and majestically among us with an object containing an image of the Medicine Buddha. But first he instructed us that he would touch our head and our hands with this object, and then we were, with our own hands, to touch our throat, heart, navel, and genitals. So each of us, having been blessed by this venerable man in robes, solemnly touched our bodies, including our genitals, as he passed by. As I put my hands on my own genitals, I thought how odd this would seem in a Catholic church. But for the Tibetan Buddhists, it was gravely important that one's whole being receive the empowering influence of the blessing.

Sex and Reality

Fundamental consciousness is our true nature, the dimension of authenticity. When we bring this dimension into our sexual intimacy, we experience authentic connection with each other. As in all aspects of life, everyone wants to be authentic in sex, but it is not so easy. From our earliest years, our family, friends, and culture teach us very specific ideas about what sex should be like and what men and women should be like during sex. The whole event, from seduction to the sex act itself, is often, as erotic writer Marco Vassi described it, a "little bit of theater."[4] We are prepared for our roles in this production long before we can make an informed choice in the matter. By the time we are adults, the characters that we play and the attitudes that we project toward potential lovers can easily be mistaken for our true nature, because they have become chronic holding patterns in our body.

As children and adolescents, we distort our bodies to conform to the "attitude" of femaleness or maleness that we see in our parents, teachers, and media stars. For example, boys may mimic the aloof, stoic quality of the men they admire by literally locking themselves up within their bodies, constricting their emotional responses until they truly become as cool and alienated as most of our male cultural heroes. Or they may chronically inflate their chests or thrust forward with their heads in an imitation of aggressive male authority. During sex, this male stereotype is compelled to maintain both dominance and self-control. In relationship with a woman who has been taught to passively receive the sexual event, his role becomes a high-stakes solo.

A woman may chronically constrict her intellect in order to make herself more "approachable," and tighten her throat to stop expressions of opinion or anger. She may try to conform to the standard image of feminine sexual allure by chronically holding in her stomach muscles, lifting her chest, and exaggerating the protrusion of her behind. In the movie *Female Perversions,* based on the book by psychologist Louise J. Kaplan, a woman explains to a young girl that she did not know how to be feminine when she was young. As the girl watches in fascination and horror, the woman gyrates her hips in a graceless, exaggerated dance of seduction. "It takes a while to get it, but you will," she promises, with just a hint of threat in her voice. Almost all girls grow up objectifying their bodies, presenting a prepared image of themselves to the appraising gaze of the world while they hide out elsewhere. They become the object rather than the subject. In order to be a successful object during sex, a woman must continue to project a sexy image, which may entirely distract her from experiencing her actual sexual sensation.

As we grow up learning the artifices of the men and women around us, we also imprint the troubled ways in which these two characters relate with each other. One of the most common patterns of misinteraction can be described as the relationship between a sponge and a stone. The woman, open and responsive emotionally but feeling no sense of her own existence, looks desperately to her male partner for the emotional response she believes she needs in order to feel alive. The man, already conditioned to suppress his emotions, feels that his own life substance is threatened by the absorbing neediness of the woman, and barricades himself against her demands with all of his will. This catch-22 of male-female relationship has dire consequences in the arena of sexual intimacy. There can be no contact or energetic flow, no exchange of pleasure, between a stone and a sponge.

Another type of confusion generated by the encounter of male and female images was illustrated by a married couple who came to work with me last year. In the first session, they volleyed a multitude of complaints against each other, which could be reduced to two main and somewhat contradictory themes. Sylvia was upset by her husband's fondness for pornography and his ogling of attractive women whenever they went out together. "He's attracted to body parts," she told me with a sneer. Simon's main complaint was his wife's obsession with her appearance. "She has to put on makeup to mail a letter half a block from our house. She has to try three outfits on before we can go out, and I'm supposed to tell her how great she looks in them. If I make any criticism at all, we never get out the door."

Sylvia was particularly hurt by Simon's looking at other women. Her response was complex, she said. She felt that she could not measure up to the women that Simon admired, and she also felt "chilled" that his attention could be claimed by something as "impersonal" as a well-shaped body. Simon felt that Sylvia was overreacting. He said that all men looked at women; it was perfectly natural and had no bearing on his feelings for Sylvia.

This conflict between them also affected their sexual intimacy. Sylvia said that Simon was "in some sort of daze" when they made love. "He looks away, it's as if he's not even really touching me." Simon asked what she meant by this, and Sylvia explained, "I can tell that you don't really feel me when you touch me." Simon complained that Sylvia was also in "some other state" during sex. "It's like she's putting on an act. She makes all kinds of sounds, but it's not really sexy because it doesn't seem real." This made

Sylvia furious. Who was he, she asked, to talk about reality? She was just trying to make herself seem sexier because she knew she was competing with some fantasy in his head about the ideal woman. She accused him of fantasizing about other women when they made love. "Admit it," she demanded. At this Simon looked embarrassed and conceded that he usually did picture a woman that he had seen in a magazine or on the street.

"It just makes it more exciting," he said.

"Not for me," Sylvia countered.

They kept returning to this theme in the following sessions, and it became clear that this was the major source of discord in their relationship. Simon continued to ridicule Sylvia's concern about her appearance, and Sylvia continued to complain about Simon's attentions to other women. Then one day they came to their session in a particular state of fury. They had gotten to my town a little early and had gone to a coffee shop nearby. The young waitress serving them was wearing a mini-skirt, and Simon had apparently followed her with his eyes as she went about her work during the whole twenty minutes or so that they were in the restaurant. "He doesn't just look," Sylvia told me. "It's as if he's fixated. Otherwise he would know he was hurting my feelings and stop. I mean, he can look all he wants when we're not together. But once he's focused on some woman, it's as if I'm not even there. He can't control it. And it doesn't even matter how pretty the woman is. He responds to the act."

She looked at me to see if I knew what she meant by "the act." I did. Instead of the angry rejoinder that I expected from Simon, he looked thoughtful. "I guess that's true," he said. "It is like a fixation. That's why I don't like when you dress up like that."

"Why?" asked Sylvia.

"Because I feel manipulated. Like I have to respond in a certain way."

This is another unhappy paradox of conventional male-female

relationships. Men often feel manipulated by the constant barrage of erotic female images served up in the media and imitated by girls and women. But women try to become these images because men respond to them. The extreme sexual objectification of women gives rise to the image of woman as both slave and manipulator of men, and to the image of man as both dominator and victim of women. Although it most likely is natural for heterosexual men to look at women and for women to enjoy the attention of men, the cultural exaggeration of this motif creates an artificial posturing on both sides that obscures our actual attraction to each other.

Simon described feeling pleasantly "fed" by the women he stared at in magazines or on the street. But he was also aware of anger toward them, anger at feeling pushed toward sexual arousal by their eroticized mannerisms, and at the expectation of response that was the measure of his manhood. He also resented having to reassure Sylvia about her appearance, and he felt confused and guilty about his awareness of her physical flaws. Sylvia, for her part, felt insecure about her ability to compete with the attractiveness of the women Simon looked at, even though she recognized their sexuality as contrived and superficial. She knew that she would never have the perfect body that Simon seemed to be looking for, and she feared that as she aged, she would lose his attention altogether.

As Simon and Sylvia began to discuss these issues with each other, they realized that they were both trapped in the same cultural myth. In order to heal their relationship, they needed to see through these images of male and female seduction to the actual sexuality of their own bodies. Simon found that by allowing himself to look clearly at the women around him, he could free himself of the manipulation of their sexy "act." Sylvia discovered that by inhabiting her own body, particularly her sexual anatomy, she had an ongoing felt sense of her true attractiveness.

Many people fear that if they let go of their gender image, they will no longer be attractive to the opposite sex. Stereotypical behaviors, for example an attitude of dimwittedness or helplessness in women or an attitude of authority or invulnerability in men, are like codes that we have learned to convey sexual appeal. For actual contact to occur between people, it is necessary to trade these codes for the specificity of real communication, to go beyond the beaming of images to the actual encounter of two human beings. The courage for this shift emerges out of spiritual love, by which I mean the love of reality. When we inhabit our gender as a quality of being, rather than as theater, we may not draw the attention of every man or woman we meet, but we will attract those people who truly excite us.

Exercises

The following four exercises can help you develop your sexual contact with each other. They can also help address specific sexual difficulties such as overstimulation or underarousal. Exercises 14 and 17 can help you and your partner use your sexual intimacy to mature your realization of fundamental consciousness. My only word of caution about these exercises is not to let them replace your sexual life together. They are just exercises. Both sex and spiritual realization are about letting go. All of the exercises in this book are meant to help you let go more deeply and subtly.

EXERCISE 14 DEVELOPING CONTACT DURING SEX

Partners should touch each other's hands (palm to palm). Maintaining this touch, feel that you inhabit your own hand. Feel how this changes the quality of contact between you. Let yourselves experience the contact between your hands.

Experience that you inhabit your lips. Feel the contact of your upper lip against your lower lip.

Still inhabiting your own lips, touch your lips to your partner's lips. Experience the contact between your lips. Slowly move your lips along your partner's lips, maintaining contact.

Partners can practice this exercise with any parts of the body.

Experience that you inhabit your genitals. Touch your genitals to your partner's genitals. Heterosexual couples should practice this with the man's penis inside of the woman's vagina. Experience the contact between your genitals. Practice maintaining this contact while moving your genitals against your partner's genitals.

Either standing up or lying down, feel that you inhabit your whole body all at once.

Staying inside your own body, touch the whole front of your body to your partner's body. Experience the contact between your bodies. Staying within your own body, experience that you contact the whole internal space of your partner's body.

EXERCISE 15 THE "SECRET" CHAKRA

Tibetan Buddhism mentions an important chakra, called the "secret" chakra, for intensifying sexual pleasure. It is located at the tip of the penis and at the top of the vagina. You can develop this chakra by penetrating into it with your focus and breathing within it. Let your breath be very subtle (it feels like a mixture of breath and mind) as you do this.

Before you begin practicing this exercise, you should be proficient in the exercise of breathing within the subtle core of the body, described in chapter 3. This will help develop your ability to bring a precise focus into this part of your body and experience subtle breath there.

EXERCISE 16 STRENGTHENING THE PC MUSCLE

This exercise strengthens the pubococcygeal muscle at the base of the torso. Most experts on sexuality agree that the strength of this muscle is crucial for sexual pleasure in both men and women. You can locate this muscle by imagining that you are stopping the flow of urine. Then contract and release this area, beginning with just a few repetitions at a time and progressing to as many as feels comfortable. This exercise becomes more powerful if you inhale on the contraction, hold your breath and the contraction as long as you can comfortably, and then release your breath and the muscle at the same time.

EXERCISE 17 CORE ATTUNEMENT DURING SEX

This is the main spiritual sex exercise of the Realization Process. It can help free the upward energy through the subtle core of the body and bring both partners into the dimension of spiritual oneness.

Lie facing each other, with either partner on top or with both of you on your sides. Heterosexual partners can do the exercise with the man's penis inside the woman's vagina.

Both partners follow these instructions at the same time.

Experience that you are inside your whole body all at once. Find the space outside your body. Experience that the space pervading your body also pervades the body of your partner. Be sure to remain inside your own body as you do this.

Maintain your attunement to fundamental consciousness pervading both your bodies as you begin stimulating each other through genital contact and movement.

When you are both aroused, stop moving and find your first chakra, at the base of your spine. Bring your focus deeply and precisely within the subtle core of the first chakra. From your own first chakra, find your partner's first chakra. Stay in your own first chakra as you do this.

Find the "secret" chakra at the tip of the penis or the top of the vagina. Bring your focus precisely into this point. From this chakra, find the corresponding chakra of your partner.

Find your second chakra, in the innermost core of your sacral area. From your own second chakra, find your partner's second chakra. Experience the energy of your sexual arousal move up through your core to your second chakra. Do not pull the energy upward; the energy will rise upward by itself if you open to it. If this does not happen right away, it will with practice.

Find your third chakra, on the level of your navel but in the subtle core of your body. From your own third chakra, find your partner's third chakra. Experience the energy of your sexual arousal move up through your core to your third chakra.

If you lose your sensation of sexual arousal, begin again to stimulate each other through genital contact and movement. When you feel sufficiently aroused, you can continue the attunement exercise.

Find your heart chakra, in the innermost subtle core of your chest. From your own heart chakra, find your partner's heart chakra. Experience the energy of your sexual arousal move up through your core to your heart chakra.

Find your throat chakra, in the innermost subtle core of your throat. From your own throat chakra, find your partner's throat chakra. Experience the energy of your sexual arousal move up through your core to your throat chakra.

Find the center of your head. From the center of your head, find the center of your partner's head. Experience the energy of your sexual arousal move up through your core to the center of your head.

Find your seventh chakra, at the center of the top of your head. From your own seventh chakra, find your partner's seventh chakra. Experience the energy of your sexual arousal move up through your whole core to your seventh chakra.

VIII

MILLER ROAD
Love and the
Spiritual Path

The subtle source is clear and bright;
the tributary streams flow through the darkness.

THE SANDOKAI

IT IS THIRTY YEARS since Zoran and I first listened to the crickets together at the Zen monastery. We still live in the mountains of upstate New York, surrounded by forest and wild creatures. Deer, turkeys, rabbits, coyotes, and the occasional black bear dance across the field in front of our home. Birds sing in the trees and glide through the high, luminous sky. It occurs to me as I look out at this extravagant display of nature that I now have abundantly and easily what I have glimpsed and strained to catch hold of since I was a child.

I remember the one tree that I could see from my bedroom window when I was growing up. I would sit on my bed and contemplate the vitality that seemed to speak to me from within its branches. In the summer, on short trips to the country, I felt the trees communing with each other in the same silent language. If I made myself quiet enough, I could join in the conversation. As I grew older, I found that there were a few people with whom I could also feel this subtle, potent connection. I remember the first time I felt the inside of my chest communicating with the inside of another person's chest in the same wordless voice as the trees.

I began performing as a dancer when I was ten. When I danced, I found that I could fill my body with this voice; I could become the language of the trees and feel its communion with the same mysterious element in the audience. But as I grew up, I forced myself to meet the rigorous technical demands required by the dance company that I performed with. My body became rigid and objectified, somehow separate from my constant, stern appraisal of it.

When I arrived at the Zen monastery in 1981, I was still recovering from an injury that had ended my life as a dancer almost a decade before. A severe dislocation of my spine and subsequent surgery had cost me my means of expressing myself, my physical well-being and strength, and my community of friends, most of whom were dancers, along with the man I lived with, who had no interest in going into this newly dark, disabled place with me.

All of my carefully organized images of my body, world, and future fell away. At first, there seemed to be nothing left. Then, very gradually, the darkness revealed its core of light. It was only as I began the long, slow process of healing that I understood how imbalanced and cut off from reality I had become.

Everyone in the modern world has probably heard that there is no absolute reality, that truth is relative. This relative nature of reality is particularly valued today, as our recognition of it allows us to debunk and discard old tyrannies and social hierarchies. No human being can say what is right and true for everyone because we each interpret events according to our personal history and culture. And yet there *is* a reality that we twist away from and that we can return to. One of the main Hindu prayers petitions God to "lead me from untruth to truth." This truth is a dimension of reality beyond the interpretation of meanings, beyond the workings of the individual thinking mind. It is the spiritual essence, the radiant, sentient transparency, pervading everywhere. When we can access this reality, we are truly in contact with ourselves, with nature, and with other human beings.

After several weekend retreats at the monastery, I decided to devote myself full time to spiritual practice. I had already made several visits to India, looking for some miracle of physical healing but finding instead the very slow, steady healing of my heart. I always came home from these trips determined to pick up my dancing life again, only to be forced to admit that my body was far from ready. So one autumn day, I gave up my loft in New York City and moved upstate. It was a radical change, from the clatter and racket of the city to the silence and stillness of the mountain landscape. The monastery seemed to me to be perched at the edge of the world, surrounded by vibrant wilderness. But having lost the sensation of grace in own my body, I felt spiritually bereft and estranged from the beauty around me.

Every day, the monastery residents had to work in the monastery. By some amazing luck, I was given the job of collecting and arranging the flowers for the many altars in the building. So while the rest of the sangha was busy dusting and vacuuming and cleaning toilets, I was outside in the forest, peering into each wildflower, examining each bit of brush and grass for its place in the altar vases. Very gradually, I was welcomed back into nature. I remembered the old language.

It was shortly after I moved to the monastery that I met Zoran. I had been alone for many years and had some vague sense that I might find a husband at the monastery. I pictured someone slightly older than myself, a doctor possibly, someone with a solid, well-established life. Zoran was twelve years younger than me, spoke barely any English, had no job to speak of, and dressed in the ill-fitting clothes from the "free store" in the monastery basement. At thirty-four, still stunned from the shattering of my life, I wasn't the lover that he had in mind, either. But from our very first meeting, there seemed to be a bond between us that could not be broken.

Miller Road runs parallel to the monastery property, along a creek. Zoran and I took many walks along Miller Road during the year that we spent there, puzzling together over the strange Eastern teachings that we were studying. It felt as if we were returning to an old conversation, as if we had been walking next to each other for millennia. As the year progressed and our meditation practice deepened, the space between us opened. I felt, for the first time in my life, that I could be both in my own body and deeply connected to another person. It was both further away and closer to someone than I had ever been.

I was sitting on a rock in the creek along Miller Road when I first noticed a strange weightlessness to everything around me. My own body seemed to be made of space, and everything I saw was also made of space. I was struck by the absolute unity of sky, mountains, forest, and water. One space. Not just around what I was seeing, but throughout it. Every day that I had lived at the monastery, we had chanted in monotone: "Form is emptiness, emptiness is form." Now, here it was. As I walked back to the monastery, I recognized that this empty space, this transparency, was even more subtle than the silent language of the forest, than the communication between forms.

After about a year, living in a monastery became less tolerable for me. Everything that I had loved about monastic life, the unchanging schedule of rituals and meditation, the small community of residents, the sense of isolation from the rest of the world, now seemed confining. Zoran and I had grown apart in those last months, and I did not think we had much future together. I decided to rent a little house in the nearby town of Woodstock. Before I left, I went up to Zoran's room to get a book that I had lent him. Since he wasn't there and I couldn't find my book, I opened a drawer of his dresser. As I bent down to look for the book, a wave of love rose up from his shirts and streamed into my chest.

Several weeks later, Zoran also moved to Woodstock. I ran into him at the health-food store, and he told me that his student visa was expiring. A woman had agreed to marry him so that he could get his green card and stay in the country. They were meeting the next day to get blood tests. I felt some shock at this news, but I said to him, as lightly as I could, "Well, if she doesn't show up, I will marry you." The next evening, I found him outside my door. The woman had not shown up for the blood test. We were married the following month.

Although by now we have walked down many roads together, we sometimes go back and walk the length of Miller Road. We have grown far from the injured dancer and the poor immigrant that we were when we first met. As we walk next to each other, I feel the deepened ground in us, the gravity. Although more involved now with worldly concerns than we were three decades ago, we are also more transparent. The meeting of our hands touches everywhere in our bodies. Our thoughts and feelings and sensations move fluidly between us. We are both more separate from each other and more connected than we have ever been. There have been many challenges along the way. Many times, painfully, we have had to stretch our understanding and our capacity to love in order to stay together. Each time has increased the depth and pleasure of our contact with each other.

There is an Indian story of a king who was looking for a spiritual teacher. Many renowned sages and scholars applied for the position, but the king rejected them. Finally one man, humble in appearance and seemingly out of place in the rich court, approached the throne. Instead of expounding his spiritual knowledge, the man looked deeply into the king's eyes. The king knelt before this man and began to weep. He had found his teacher.

Human beings know instinctively that the ability to love is more valuable than any other type of accomplishment. The path of personal and spiritual growth leads toward the ability for genuine contact. This is a transformation of our entire organism. The body softens and becomes available for pleasure, the heart opens and becomes available for feeling, and the mind clears and becomes available for understanding. We no longer meet the world at the surface of ourselves, but through the subtle, internal depth of our whole being. As we learn the spiritual lessons of compassion and nongrasping, as we trace our way backward through the labyrinth of our psychological defenses, as we attune inward to the subtlest essence of our being, we are transformed into lovers of life.

Acknowledgments

TO ALL of my friends, family, teachers, and students who, by your presence in my life, helped me open my heart; every page of this book was written because of you. And to Zoran, who has helped melt some of the stoniest barriers in my heart: thank you for your persistence and courage on the path of love. And thank you to the whole staff at Sounds True, an extraordinary company founded on love.

Notes

CHAPTER 1   The Relational Field

1 Robert D. Stolorow, George E. Atwood, *Contexts of Being* (Hillsdale, NJ: The Analytic Press, 1992).

2 Sankara, *Self-Knowledge,* trans. Swami Nikhilananda (New York: Ramakrishna-Vivekananda Center, 1974), 149.

3 Longchen Rabjam, *A Treasure Trove of Spritual Transmission,* trans. R. Barron (Junction City, CA: Padma Publishing, 2001), 151.

4 Lama Thubten Yeshe writes, "With achievement of the illusory body, a very high attainment, there is total unity of body and mind." *The Bliss of Inner Fire* (Boston: Wisdom Publications, 1998), 84.

5 Jim Dodge, *Fup* (Berkeley, CA: City Miner Books, 1983), 44.

CHAPTER 2   Oneness and Separateness

1 R. D. Laing, *The Divided Self* (Tavistock, 1959; Baltimore, MD: Penguin, 1965), 52–53, quoted in Judith Blackstone, *The Enlightenment Process* (Boston: Element, 1997), 75–76.

2 Margaret Mahler, *The Psychological Birth of the Human Infant* (New York: Bantam Books, 1975).

3 Daniel N. Stern, *The Interpersonal World of the Infant* (New York: Basic Books, 1985).

CHAPTER 4   Mutual Contact

1 Shunryu Suzuki, *Zen Mind, Beginner's Mind* (New York: Weatherhill, 1980), 41.

2 Manjusrimitra, *Primordial Experience,* trans. Namkhai Norbu, Kennard Lipman (Boston: Shambhala, 1987), xiii.

3 Tsele Natsok Rangdrol, *The Circle of the Sun,* trans. Erik Pema Kunsang (Hong Kong: Rangjung Yeshe Publications, 1990), 72.

4 Harville Hendrix, *Getting the Love You Want* (New York: Harper Perennial, 1988).

CHAPTER 5   Bare Perception

1 Bhikkhu Nanananda, *Concept and Reality in Early Buddhist Thought* (Kandy, Sri Lanka: Buddhist Publication Society, 1971), 30.

2 Toshihiko Izutsu, *Toward a Philosophy of Zen Buddhism* (Boulder, CO: Prajna Press, 1982), 39.

3 Meir Schneider, *Self Healing: My Life and Vision* (New York: Routledge & Kegan Paul, 1987).

4 Lex Hixon, *Mother of the Buddhas* (Wheaton, IL: Quest Books, 1993), 246–47.

CHAPTER 6   Compassion

1 Terrence Real, *I Don't Want To Talk About It* (New York: Fireside, 1997), 130.

CHAPTER 7   Sexual Intimacy

1 The traditional and Realization Process sex exercises are effective for both heterosexual and same-sex partners. Any two people who experience the excitement of sexual arousal can apply that excitement to spiritual realization.

2 Lama Thubten Yeshe, *The Bliss of Inner Fire* (Somerville, MA: Wisdom Publications, 1998), 166.

3 Thomas Merton, *The Asian Journal of Thomas Merton* (New York: New Directions Books, 1968), 66.

4 Marco Vassi, *Woodstock Times,* circa 1981.

About the Author

JUDITH BLACKSTONE, PhD, developed the Realization Process, an innovative integration of nondual spiritual awakening, psychological healing, and embodiment. She offers workshops and teacher trainings in the Realization Process throughout the United States and Europe. She is a psychotherapist in New York City and author of *The Empathic Ground, The Enlightenment Process,* and *The Subtle Self.* She is the founding director of the Nonduality Institute in New York City.

Judith began performing at age ten with a modern dance company in New York City. She danced for fifteen years until a back injury brought her to the spiritual path. She has been a meditation practitioner for almost four decades, studying with Hindu, Zen, and Tibetan Buddhist teachers. The Realization Process emerged outside of traditional lineages, in response to the needs of contemporary seekers. For more information on the Realization Process, visit judithblackstone.com.

About Sounds True

SOUNDS TRUE is a multimedia publisher whose mission is to inspire and support personal transformation and spiritual awakening. Founded in 1985 and located in Boulder, Colorado, we work with many of the leading spiritual teachers, thinkers, healers, and visionary artists of our time. We strive with every title to preserve the essential "living wisdom" of the author or artist. It is our goal to create products that not only provide information to a reader or listener, but that also embody the quality of a wisdom transmission.

For those seeking genuine transformation, Sounds True is your trusted partner. At SoundsTrue.com you will find a wealth of free resources to support your journey, including exclusive weekly audio interviews, free downloads, interactive learning tools, and other special savings on all our titles.

To listen to a podcast interview with Sounds True publisher Tami Simon and author Judith Blackstone, please visit SoundsTrue.com/bonus/Judith_Blackstone_Realize. You can also hear a guided exercise, "Attuning to Fundamental Consciousness," at the same Web address.

SOUNDS TRUE
many voices, one journey